UNBREAKABLE

The SEVEN PILLARS of
a KINGDOM FAMILY

UNBREAKABLE

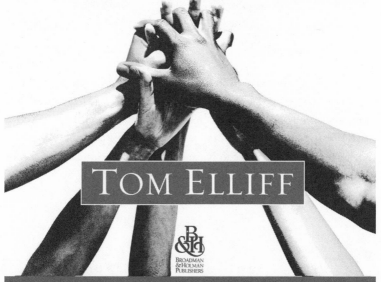

TOM ELLIFF

B&H
BROADMAN
&HOLMAN
PUBLISHERS

Nashville, Tennessee

Published by Broadman & Holman Publishers
Nashville, Tennessee

Dewey Decimal Classification: 306.85
Subject Heading: FAMILY LIFE \ PARENT AND CHILD

1 2 3 4 5 6 7 8 9 10   08 07 06 05 04 03

Dedicated
To the Members of First Southern Baptist Church,
Del City, Oklahoma,
My Church Family,
Whose Prayerful Support and Encouragement
Have Made This Book Possible.
Thank You for Seeking to Build Your Homes
on These
Seven Pillars of a Kingdom Family.

"Wisdom has built her house,
She has hewn out her seven pillars."

PROVERBS 9:1

TABLE OF CONTENTS

WITH GRATITUDE

A project like this comes to fruition because many besides this author are willing to bear part of the load. I cannot allow the opportunity to pass without expressing my deep love and appreciation to Jeannie, my wife of thirty-seven years, mother of our four children and grandmother to eighteen (and counting!). She is my heart's trusted companion and fellow pilgrim on the journey.

Our children have been of enormous help as we have discussed whether what Dad and Mom say works, really does. They have each contributed to a previous book written by us entitled *Letters to Lovers.* They are a benediction to us.

Jennifer Wilson, the pastor's administrative assistant at First Southern Baptist Church in Del City, Oklahoma, is both talented and tireless, a real trooper whose encouragement regarding this project helped us all to keep on track. In reality, she typifies the entire team at First Southern, folks who know how to love, support, challenge, and work for the Kingdom's sake.

Thanks also to David Shepherd and Len Goss at Broadman & Holman. They conceived the idea for this book in connection with the work of the Southern Baptist Council on Family Life. Thanks, guys, for all your help and encouragement. I've enjoyed working with you.

Dr. Paige Patterson and his team of theologians from Southeastern Baptist Theological Seminary gave willingly of their time and counsel as we sought to hammer out the best wording for the Seven Pillars. Your labor and thoughtfulness are not forgotten.

I have difficulty adequately expressing my appreciation to the members of the Southern Baptist Council on Family Life. They have been my teammates for over two years now as we have developed the strategy for Empowering Kingdom Families. Thanks Bob Oxford, Forrest Pollock, Danny Aikens, Marcia Coleman, Jim Futrall, Ruffin Snow, Mike Hand, and Augie Boto. You have given tirelessly of yourselves, and my life is the richer for our relationship. Only time and eternity will properly record the impact of your prayers and work.

Our council originated as a result of the heart cry issued to our entire Southern Baptist Convention by our chief executive, Dr. Morris H. Chapman, a plea to "save the family." Now his vision has become ours, yours, and mine as many have rallied to his appeal. Thanks, Morris, for this challenge and for your friendship and prayers.

INTRODUCTION

This book is about a movement that is gaining momentum with each passing day. It is a movement to rescue and restore the family to God's intended purpose. It is a movement to raise up families that will make a positive spiritual difference in the world. Stated simply, it is a movement that calls upon each of us to build our lives and homes on *The Seven Pillars of a Kingdom Family*. The end result is a life, and a family, that honors God, lives out His principles, effectively carries the gospel to the nations, and passes along a legacy of faith to succeeding generations.

This is not a book merely for those facing issues at a particular age or stage in life. Nor is it a book for the married rather than the unmarried. It is a book for students, grandparents, husbands, wives, children, singles, and yes, single parents. It is a book for those whose lives have been, until now, sadly spent in rebellion against God and His principles. It is for those who desperately are seeking hope and help for their lives and families. And it is a book for those who have been blessed with a deeply committed and spiritual heritage. It is for those whose marriages and families are solid and who want to keep them that way. It is a book for anyone desiring to pass along a legacy of faith to the next generation. In other words, this book was written specifically with *you* in mind.

In the following pages you will find an invitation to join this movement as a member of God's Kingdom Family, and you will discover the practical help you need to make that possible. You will find how you can experience a fresh new touch of God's Spirit, new strength for the journey, and a new level of excitement and encouragement. You will discover that if you are *for* the family, God is *for* you.

FOR BEST RESULTS

I remember once reading the instructions on the side of a can of paint. They included some hints for achieving the best results. I want to do the same for you as you begin reading this book.

First, read each chapter thoroughly. Those who race through the following pages will receive no prize. In fact, you may receive no benefit at all. So read each chapter with a listening ear. What applications would God have you make of the information you are reading? How can you get started?

Second, be honest in your answers to the questions at the end of each chapter. After all, God is the grader, and He knows the correct answers. Unless asked to do so, don't answer the questions as you know they should be answered, as you once would have answered them, or as you would like to answer them. Don't answer on the basis of what you intend to do in the future. Just be honest! OK?

Third, it would be great to go through this book with an accountability partner. If you are married and your spouse would agree to fulfill that role, that's the best possible scenario for you. Are you engaged? Then your future spouse could be the perfect accountability partner. But be sure you don't hide anything or pull any punches. The truth will one day come out, so why not just spill the beans now? Your future partner doesn't need to marry what once was called "a pig in a poke"—buying a pig in a sack without first knowing the state of its health. Single? Find a disciplined, believing friend and work together through these pages. Are you a student? Then do the same. Or maybe you can convince your folks to go on the journey with you. Talk about a refreshing experience!

FOR PASTORS, MARRIAGE, AND PREMARRIAGE COUNSELORS

In reality, this book contains a summary of the material I have faithfully used for more than twenty-eight years in counseling, both premarriage and marriage. When conducting premarriage counseling, for instance, I explain in the initial session that the couple must embrace certain principles and determine to employ them in their marriage *if* we are to proceed. I carefully review with them what we are now calling *The Seven Pillars of a Kingdom Family.* I ask them not to answer me in that initial session but to spend time in prayer over these principles. If they find they are willing to embrace these principles fully, I ask the groom to call and schedule the next premarriage session. Those sessions which follow take place over a period of approximately four months prior to the marriage ceremony. In these sessions, I deal in detail with each of the Seven Pillars.

On occasion, fellow pastors have challenged this approach, saying, for instance, that requiring both bride and groom to have experienced genuine salvation and be engaged in a dynamic practice of their faith eliminates the opportunity to minister to them over the long haul. On the contrary, if I were to marry a couple in direct contradiction to proven scriptural principles, I would forfeit my opportunity to minister to them at all.

As a matter of record, as I have taken time to share these convictions, I have had the opportunity to lead many grooms and brides to the Lord and often their parents as well. I personally instituted these principles in 1974 after an informal study lasting two years. As of this writing, I actually know of only three couples whose marriages I have performed who have subsequently divorced. This is not a scientific survey (I am confident there must be or will be others), but that statistic is singularly significant since most of these marriages have been performed in communities where the divorce rate far outstrips the rate of marriage. (In the case of two of the aforementioned couples, either the bride or groom has subsequently told me that they twisted the truth in our counseling sessions and had no intention of living by the principles as agreed.)

In marriage counseling with couples, I have found it helpful to employ these same Seven Pillars, beginning by establishing whether each, in fact, possesses genuine salvation. Then as we work through these principles one at a time, the couples often experience a moment of truth when they see how their difficulties are directly related to specific disobedience in one or more areas. After that, genuine healing takes place through confession, repentance, and restoration.

IT'S A JOURNEY,
NOT A DANCE!

There's a vast difference between a journey and a dance. Once the dance is over, you're pretty much where you started. But on a journey each step takes you closer to the goal. And the goal is a life, both a personal and a family life, that honors God, lives out His principles, brings the gospel to the nations, and passes along a legacy of faith to each succeeding generation.

Welcome to the journey! You're going to have a great time building your life and home on *The Seven Pillars of a Kingdom Family.* Your world will be different because of it. You are becoming part of a movement that will change your life, strengthen your home, revolutionize your church and community, and reach the nations for Christ. Together with others, in prayerful dependence on the grace of God and for His eternal glory, it's time to give yourself to building God's Kingdom Family!

Yours for Kingdom Families,
Tom Elliff

I am a member of God's Kingdom Family. I have by faith repented of my sin, believed on Christ as my Lord and Savior, and received His gift of forgiveness and eternal life. By the miracle of God's grace, I am both a citizen of His kingdom and a member of His family, His subject and His child, His bond slave and a joint heir with Him, His battle-ready soldier and His bride. It is now my desire to glorify the Lord by giving my own earthly family relationships the interest and care they so richly deserve. With the balance of my life and relying on the leadership of God's Spirit, I will commit to God's plan for my life and family.

CHAPTER ONE

WRONG FOUNDATIONS, WRECKED FAMILIES

The summer heat, beat back by the straining air conditioner, was no match for the discussion being carried on in the living room. I had visited in the home before but never under these circumstances. A seemingly stable, faithful family was falling apart.

The children had been packed off to their grandparents for less than an hour when the argument began. When words like *divorce* and phrases like *no love left in my heart* began to be thrown about like the punches of a desperate boxer, the grieving wife had picked up the phone and called the preacher. Now I was bargaining for a delay, a calmness, an opportunity to see what God could do.

I don't remember everything I said in my attempt to buy time for a miracle. But I do remember standing on the couple's front porch as I was preparing to leave. I was trying my best to convey some sense of hope. In a lame attempt to change subjects, the husband pointed to a crack in the brick veneer, a crack I traced, first up to the roofline, then as it meandered all the way to the foundation, which had also settled and cracked. Here was a house that would be hard to sell if a divorce occurred. Who wants a house with a poor foundation?

That house with its settling foundation and cracking veneer was the least of their worries. Their home was in a far more serious condition than their house. The pressures of life were revealing the simple fact that this family, like the house in which they lived, was built on something other than a solid foundation. Now the cracks were numerous and exaggerated. The couple despaired of ever finding a way to repair them.

THE HIDDEN IMPERATIVE

Nothing is more critical to a building than its foundation. Everything rests upon it. Beautiful buildings have been abandoned because they rested on poor foundations. I once saw a cartoon that depicted two stone masons, trowels in hand, discussing a building being erected immediately behind them. "I skimped a little on the foundation," said one, "but no one will ever notice." A closer look revealed the building to be none other than what would ultimately be known as the Leaning Tower of Pisa!

In our haste to see visible progress, we often overlook the importance of the foundation, which is hidden. Once ground is broken, the time it then takes to get a building out of the ground seems interminable. But no thinking person will deny that, though ultimately hidden, the foundation is a matter of critical importance. Failure to consider this simple fact ensures the ultimate ruin of what is built upon it.

"WE GOT MARRIED IN A FEVER"

A once-popular pop duet opened with an admission that the lovers married "in a fever." They were not alone. Today's crumbling marriages are evidence that, more often than not, couples enter marriage with little time given to the foundation upon which they hope to build a union that will last a lifetime. Good homes, like good houses, both require and deserve a proper foundation.

Marriage ceremonies can involve an incredible expenditure of time, energy, emotion, and—oh yes—money. Doesn't the institution of marriage itself deserve at least equal time? After all, the ceremony is just the initial celebration for what is meant to be a lifetime of happiness. Shouldn't appropriate consideration be given to the foundation upon which the future will be built?

More than twenty-eight years ago, I began insisting that any couple who requested that I conduct their marriage ceremony must agree to participate in at least three-and-a-half to four months of premarital counseling. In the initial session I discuss with them the scriptural prerequisites for marriage, focusing on this simple fact: Since marriage is God's idea and God's institution, it is imperative that the bride and groom each know Christ as Savior *and* possess a vital, dynamic relationship with Him as Lord. Given the current proliferation of divorce, the results of this insistence—and the required counseling—have been nothing less than astounding! When a couple is determined to start out right and build on God's principles, they are on the road to a relationship that can stand all the tests life throws at it.

CHOOSING THE RIGHT FOUNDATION

No marriage can possibly be all God intends unless both husband and wife possess an intimate, saving relationship with Christ, a relationship that brings them together in the experiences of prayer, worship, and faithful service to Him. This is the foundation upon which everything else in the marriage must be built. Fail here and the marriage will never enjoy God's best, even if the couple are still married at the end of life's journey.

This truth is simply stated in the Scripture. "For no man can lay a foundation other than the one which is laid, which is Jesus Christ" (1 Cor. 3:11 NASB). While this book is about building a Kingdom Family, it is also about choices. This one foundational choice, however, is of paramount importance: the choice to turn from your way (this is called "repentance") and to trust in Christ alone as your personal Savior. It is this choice that establishes you as a member of God's Kingdom Family and makes it possible for you successfully to build your life and family around seven key principles that we call *The Seven Pillars of a Kingdom Family*.

Does It Really Matter?

Why is it so important for two people contemplating marriage first to ensure that each has made this life-changing decision? Or as one couple once asked, "What does it really matter? After all, the only thing that matters to us is that we want to get married. All this 'trusting Christ' stuff may be important to you, and one day we may make it important to us. But why are you trying to stand in the way of our marriage by insisting that we become Christians?"

Over the next hour I explained to them why it is absolutely essential for a bride and a groom to have a dynamic personal relationship with Christ. Three reasons stand out clearly and should be considered and settled before taking the first step toward the marriage altar.

1. It's God's idea, not man's. In fact, the more humanized concepts of marriage and family become, the further they stray from God's original purpose. I recently heard a popular rock star describe his relationship with one of his many live-in lovers as "animalistic." He probably thought he was ascribing to himself a complimentary term. In reality, his use of it couldn't have been more correct. His concept of a relationship was one in which he used others for self-gratification and with no thought of their future well-being. For him, she was just one more dog along the road. Far from being complimentary, it was an admission that he, and his partners, had sunk to an animal state. Strangely, in his deluded thinking, he assumed that this made him more sophisticated.

God initiated marriage so that we could bring glory to Him, satisfy the deepest needs for human intimacy and personal growth, and ultimately to fill the earth with children who also honor Him. It is impossible to imagine fulfilling God's purpose in marriage without first knowing Him on a personal basis. Just as any book is remarkably different if you are acquainted with its author, so marriage takes on an incredibly different and exciting dimension when you know the One who thought it up in the first place.

2. *It's a covenant, not a contract.* As the institution of marriage has devolved to a mere human relationship, many participants have sought to cover their anticipated losses with the use of marriage contracts. Contracts are, at their heart, an admission that two parties cannot be trusted. After detailing what is expected of each participant, they then proceed to establish the legal recourse each can employ if the other does not fulfill the clearly spelled-out terms. In the end the court decides who wins and who loses. Of course, in a relationship like this, everybody loses.

God's plan is for marriage to be a covenant relationship. Covenants are built on trust. In the case of marriage, the two people are entering into a covenant with God, a covenant that is to last "until death do us part." In earlier days covenants were sealed by tokens. Sometimes coats, belts, or swords were exchanged as a way of indicating the nature of the covenant. Exchanged coats represented a shared identity; exchanged belts represented a shared strength; exchanged swords represented a shared determination to protect from harm. Similarly today's covenant marriages are sealed by the exchange of vows spoken "before God and these witnesses" and, in most cases, an exchange of rings.

3. *It's held together by God's love, not yours.* The Bible explains that, apart from coming to Christ for salvation, a person is "dead in trespasses and sins" (Eph. 2:1 KJV; see Ezek. 18:4). This is

not a reference to physical death or to the death of one's intellect, emotion, or will. It is a reference to the simple fact that your sin has separated you from God. In your natural state you are "dead" to God. Apart from trusting in Christ who died for all, you will forever remain that way, ultimately spending eternity in hell (Rom. 6:23a). God has made a way for you to be "born again" (John 3:3), not physically but spiritually (John 3:6). By trusting in Christ and what He did for us on the cross (2 Cor. 5:21) and through His subsequent resurrection, you may receive the "gift of God [which] is eternal life" (Rom. 6:23b). You will become forever alive to God!

When you experience the genuine salvation afforded only in Christ, you then become a channel of God's love. It is the kind of love described in 1 Corinthians 13, often called the "love chapter" of the Bible. This love that God channels through you toward those in your family is a love that "never fails." It is the kind of love upon which you can establish marriage as a covenant union rather than a contractual agreement. This love of God holds your family together!

When you enter into a personal relationship with Christ, you are establishing the foundation upon which to build a Kingdom Family, a picture of God's love for all the world to see. In fact, the manner in which you approach your own family relationships becomes a winsome, compelling argument for the gospel. Seeing what God is doing in your family through you encourages others to come to God through Christ.

WHAT IS A KINGDOM FAMILY?

Throughout this book you will see references to the Kingdom Family. While this exact term is found nowhere in the Bible, it is used in this book to describe a clearly defined biblical concept. The two most commonly employed analogies describing God's unique relationship with His people are *kingdom* and *family*. We are reminded, for instance, that we are both citizens of God's kingdom *and* joint heirs with Jesus. We belong to our King by means of His redeeming work *and* by virtue of being born again into His family.

We serve Him as His bond slaves, *and* one day we will be seated with Him as His bride. Knowing Christ, you see, establishes us as members of His Kingdom Family.

But Kingdom Family as employed in this book also refers to your personal family, both immediate and extended. It is the purpose of this book to encourage you in the establishment and building up of a family that truly pictures for all the world to see just what happens when Christ is preeminent in your life and in your family.

AS YOU ARE, WHERE YOU ARE

This book is for you, whoever you are, whatever your marital status, whatever your current spiritual condition or the spiritual condition of your family. All of us must begin our pilgrimage with Christ right where we are. This concept can be easily grasped by thinking of the gospel hymn made so famous by its use in the Billy Graham crusades. It begins with an appeal for the sinner to say, "I will come 'just as I am.'"

This is what you must do to establish the foundation upon which to build your own Kingdom Family. You must come to Christ in faith, repenting of sin and believing on Him, the One crucified for your sins and raised on the third day, as your Savior and Lord of your life. Are you building on this foundation?

Early in my own experience as a pastor, I found myself thrown into an increasing number of family situations that seemed to have no satisfactory and permanently effective answer. The fact that people were willing to come to a relatively inexperienced minister with these problems was more an indication of their desperation than my abilities! For a few years I just did my best in dishing out as much advice as I could. Most of my counsel was simply home-spun wisdom with a little Scripture thrown in for good measure. Soon I noticed that the same people were coming back again and again and again. In other words, nothing was really happening to produce change in their lives or their homes.

I remember lamenting this problem with an older pastor and personal mentor whom God had so graciously brought into my life. "You know, Tom," he commented thoughtfully, "I've discovered that most people's problems are *not* solved when they come to *me* but when they come to Christ. For that reason I never proceed with any kind of counseling, personal or family, until I am certain that they have met Christ and trusted in Him. My responsibility is showing them how to find the answers for their problems in the Word of God. But if they don't know Him and if they don't respect His Word, I'm just wasting my time and theirs."

My friend's comments make the point of this chapter: To build a Kingdom Family you must first be a member of God's own kingdom family; you must know Christ personally and be walking with Him in a dynamic, day-by-day relationship. This is the only foundation upon which you can firmly establish a meaningful and lasting marriage. And it is the only foundation upon which to build a family that can mightily impact the world for Christ.

Developing a Kingdom Family is a lifetime journey. The Word of God reminds us that "wisdom has built her house, she has hewn out her seven pillars" (Prov. 9:1). Recently I had the privilege of working with the Southern Baptist Council on Family Life as we developed what is called the Kingdom Family Commitment. Because it is the outline from which this book is developed, I wanted you to read through it here at the beginning of our journey together. It speaks about the Foundation upon which you must build and the Seven Pillars you must establish in developing a Kingdom Family.

The Kingdom Family Commitment

I am a member of God's Kingdom Family. I have repented of my sin, believed on Christ as my Lord and Savior, and received His gift of forgiveness and eternal life. By the miracle of God's grace, I am both a citizen of His kingdom and a member of His family, His subject and His child, His bond slave and a joint heir with Him,

His battle-ready soldier and His bride. It is now my desire to glorify the Lord by giving my own earthly family relationships the interest and care they so richly deserve. With the balance of my life and relying on the leadership of God's Spirit, I will commit to God's plan for my life and family by:

Honoring God's Authority

God, as Sovereign Creator and Sustainer of all, holds Ultimate Authority over His creation. By establishing the family, God has provided a unique setting in which each individual should come to understand and respect authority. I will glorify God by surrendering every area of my life to Him and by offering godly respect in all my earthly relationships, starting in my family (Rom. 12:1–2; 13:1–7; Eph. 5:21–25; 6:1–4; 1 Cor. 10:31).

Respecting Human Life

Human life is a gift from God and is of transcendent worth. It is to be treasured, protected, encouraged, and loved from the moment of conception until the moment of death. I know that each member of my family must ultimately give an account to God, and forgiveness of sin and eternal life in heaven require personal repentance of sin and faith in Christ. I will honor God by expressing self-sacrificial love to each of my family members throughout the entirety of their lives (Eph. 20:13; Ps. 119:13–16, 127–28; Prov. 16:31).

Exercising Moral Purity

God has established the family as His first institution on earth. It is worthy of my most noble aspirations and commitments, including my commitment to moral purity, marital fidelity, and Christlike love for each family member. Because marriage is a picture of Christ's faithfulness to His bride, the church, and because the family is a picture of the Father's faithfulness to His children, I will honor the Lord by being faithful and pure (Exod. 20:14; 1 Cor. 6:18–19; Job 31:1; Matt. 5:27–30).

Serving My Church

The church is the bride of Christ, comprised of all the redeemed who will, one day, be taken to heaven by Him. By exalting Christ, resting on the sufficiency of His Word, and giving place to the ministry of the Spirit, the local church becomes the means by which spiritual growth is promoted and the ministry of Christ is brought to my family, my community, and to the world. I will support and encourage my family to support our local church with faithful attendance, diligent service, generous and God-honoring giving, and loving cooperation (Matt. 16:18; Eph. 5:25; 4:11–16; Heb. 10:25).

Using Time Wisely

Time is a resource given to each person by God. My use of it, especially in matters related to my family, reflects my esteem for God. One day I will give an account to Him for how I have spent the time He entrusted to me. As I order my life in concert with His will, I will have sufficient time for personal growth through prayer, for the study of God's Word, and for fulfilling every God-given responsibility related to my family (Eph. 5:15; 2 Tim. 3:16–17; Deut. 6:6–7; Luke 18:16; Ps. 90:12).

Practicing Biblical Stewardship

God has provided material resources so that I may glorify Him through the exercise of faithful stewardship over them. I will be held accountable for this stewardship. Therefore, I will diligently seek my Master's best interests in the way I earn money, expend it for life's needs, use it to touch the lives of others, and give it for the support of His work through my local church (Luke 6:38; 12:48; Gen. 1:28; Prov. 3:9–10; 2 Cor. 9:7; 1 Cor. 4:22; 16:1–2; Mal. 3:8–11).

Sharing the Gospel of Jesus Christ

The greatest and most noble purpose in life is to glorify the Lord through the fulfillment of His Great Commission. I will glorify the Lord by sharing my faith with my family and by joining with them and others in specific activities which cultivate a passion for fulfilling the Great Commission (Matt. 28:19–20; Acts 1:8; John 4:38–39; Rom. 1:16; 1 Tim. 5:8; Rev. 22:17; Rom. 1:16).

IT WILL TAKE TIME AND HEART

There you have it! First you must establish the proper foundation. After that you can erect *The Seven Pillars of a Kingdom Family*—basic commitments that will sustain you through all the storms of life, commitments that will enable you and your family to become living illustrations of God's kingdom here on earth.

"Rome wasn't built in a day!" Neither are Kingdom Families. But the building of Rome *was* started at *one* moment on *one* day. The same is true when it comes to establishing a Kingdom Family. You must begin at some point, some moment in time, by trusting Christ as your personal Savior, choosing the right foundation. Then you are not only part of God's Kingdom Family, but you can also bring His kingdom principles into your own family.

A friend of mine says, "Life is not a science but an art." It is filled with the unanticipated, the unimaginable, and sometimes the undesired. Regardless of the circumstances life has presented, is presenting, or will present, you can enjoy success in your role as a member of God's Kingdom Family. It takes time, however, and heart!

As Henry Wadsworth Longfellow reminds us in "The Ladder of St. Augustine,"

> The heights by great men reached and kept
> Were not achieved by sudden flight,
> But they, while their companions slept,
> Were toiling upward in the night.

Building a Kingdom Family is not just a "day job." It requires choosing the right foundation and making a lifetime commitment. I am writing this book because I believe there are literally hundreds of thousands (if not millions!) of people like you who want first to be part of God's Kingdom Family and then to "flesh out" His kingdom principles right where they live!

HAVE YOU EVER SEEN ONE?

A young boy once asked his father, "Daddy, what is a Christian?" "Why, son," replied his father, "a Christian is someone who has turned from his own way and trusted Jesus as his Savior. Now Christ lives in him and gives him power over evil, victory over sin, and success over his failures. What's more, a Christian loves Jesus with all his heart, faithfully studies the Bible, prays, worships, and shares his faith. On top of all that, he has joy in his heart and loves people with the love of God." After thinking awhile about his father's answer, he said, "Daddy, has anybody ever seen one?"

I believe you want to do something more than "see" a Kingdom Family. I believe you want to be one! And it can happen in your life and in the lives of the others who mean so much to you. Recently I had the privilege of sharing Christ with a man during his stay in a local hospital. In a wonderful experience of God's grace, he opened his heart and trusted Christ as his Savior. Over the next weeks and months, a miracle took place before our eyes. His hardened heart became soft, his cursing was exchanged for praise, and his indifference was replaced by faithfulness. He said to me, "Preacher, when I got saved I lost two-thirds of my vocabulary!"

The biggest impact of this man's simple decision was felt by his family. As they saw God at work in his life, they also began to come to Christ, one by one. Months later as I preached his funeral, I was able to recognize at least six family members who had trusted in Christ. At the funeral twelve more trusted in Christ! That's the eight-month impact of a man who became part of God's Kingdom Family and wanted others to do the same.

This book is for you. Will you give the balance of your life to living as a member of God's Kingdom Family? You cannot go back and relive your past, but you can spend the rest of your life as a part of God's Kingdom Family. Where do you start? By choosing to build on the right foundation, trusting Jesus Christ as Savior and Lord over all your life!

Thinking It Through, Living It Out

1. What would family members say is the foundation upon which you are building your life? What would your friends say? What would your associates say?
2. Are there evidences in your personal life or your family life that you are building your life upon an unstable foundation? What are some of these evidences? Are there some "secret faults" that are known only by you and God?
3. If you are married, did you and your spouse settle the issue of personal faith in Christ before your marriage? Have you discussed it since becoming married? What role does faith in Christ play in your marriage? Would you describe your relationship with Him as vital, dynamic, and growing?
4. Are you confident that you have genuinely experienced God's love and forgiveness in Christ? That He lives in you? That you possess His gift of eternal life? When did you repent and believe in Him? Where were you? Are there evidences in your life today that you are a child of God? If you are unsure of your salvation, are you willing to pursue the issue immediately until it is settled?
5. Will you determine to build your life on the Seven Pillars described in the Kingdom Family Commitment? Are you willing to share that determination with your spouse (if married) and with others close to you? Will you allow them to hold you accountable for your commitment?

God, as Sovereign Creator and Sustainer of all, holds Ultimate Authority over His creation. By establishing the family, God has provided a unique setting in which each individual should properly come to understand and respect authority. I will glorify God by surrendering every area of my life to Him and by offering godly respect in all my earthly relationships, starting in my family (Rom. 12:1–2; 13:1–7; Eph. 5:21–25; 6:1–4; 1 Cor. 10:31).

Chapter Two

HONORING GOD'S AUTHORITY

It was a bitter cold night in early spring, and I was a college student serving as a "summer missionary." For that week, I was a camp counselor in northern Maine. Before I opened the door to the bunkhouse, I could hear the bedlam taking place inside. It was a free-for-all, and I was about to bring it to an end.

"Lights out!" I shouted. "Everyone get in his own bunk! Nobody gets up or goes out! And nobody is to say another word." For a moment I believe we were all surprised by the immediacy of the response. It became perfectly quiet, but only for a moment. Out of the darkness came the recognizable voice of one of my problem kids: "Are you asking us or telling us?" he queried. "I'm telling you!" I blasted back in return. "That's all I wanted to know," he said, rolling over and soon going to sleep.

His question was telling. In it there was rooted the basic issue of authority. "Who's in charge?" he was asking.

An Issue to Be Settled

From the outset any couple contemplating marriage should determine that God will occupy the position of Ultimate Authority for their family, and His Word will serve as the standard for their behavior. He will be the "glue" that holds them together, not their sensual passion (or lack of it), not their signatures on a paper authorized by a nation that one day may cease to exist, not the strength of their arguments for marriage, not the convenience of finances. It must ultimately be God and God alone who certifies their union, binds them together, guides their behavior, and blesses them. Again, it is imperative that this issue is settled.

When God delivered the Ten Commandments through Moses, He began with a reminder and a command: "I am the LORD your God, who brought you out of the land of Egypt, out of the house of bondage. You shall have no other gods before Me" (Exod. 20:2–3). Apart from our understanding and acceptance of this simple command, the other nine commandments are scarcely worth our consideration. It is an all-or-nothing proposition. It must be God, and God alone, who is the object of both worship and allegiance. He must be the Ultimate Authority in our lives.

Authority under Attack

Authority is a hot topic in each generation. It is challenged at every level and in many instances scorned by those who reject the idea that anyone other than themselves should ever be in charge. Several years ago, while traveling in mainland China, I visited with a highly educated immunologist who was reared in that country but later immigrated to the U.S. As we talked, she spoke of what she believed would become China's greatest difficulty in the years to come.

"Because of China's insistence on population control and the godless manner in which they enforce it," she said, "this nation will soon become populated by those who grew up as the only child in the family." She went on to describe how these individuals were so spoiled by their parents that they had a tendency to become self-centered and rebellious toward authority. "When that happens," said my friend, "this highly controlled society will unravel, and its population will become unmanageable."

Some say that discipline is at least 80 percent of the learning process. As national testing authorities complain about sagging scores among high school students, these questions must be asked: Are these dismal reports rooted in the contemporary disciplinary upheaval affecting so many students today? Are they an indication of our failure to understand and honor God's authority? Interestingly, these are questions many educators are hesitant to address.

One of the most disturbing trends in contemporary public education is the attempt by many to remove any reference to God from the classroom. It is not a mere coincidence that where this attempt has more or less succeeded there has been a commensurate rise in disciplinary problems. After all, if a student's respect for others is not rooted in a reverence for God, then it is reserved for those who can exert the most power, overwhelm with humanistic reason, or strongly appeal to one's naturally rebellious tendencies ("I will obey you to the extent you either impress or intimidate me").

A proper understanding of God and a corresponding reverence for Him totally changes the playing field. With this in place, an authority figure is viewed both as a person—and thereby deserving the respect due to all mankind—and as a representative of God's appointed authority. Respect becomes a matter affecting an individual's relationship with God as well as classroom behavior.

THE KINGDOM FAMILY APPROACH TO AUTHORITY

Where is this proper understanding and reverence for God to be learned? Is it the responsibility of the church? The school? The government? Yes, each of these is responsible for teaching about God, but not primarily. God intends for the family, His first institution, to be the primary setting in which each of us is to develop a proper understanding and respect for Him and for the various authority figures He places in our lives.

"God, as Sovereign Creator and Sustainer of all, holds Ultimate Authority over His creation" reads the opening line in the Kingdom Family Commitment. This is an affirmation of the first commandment, "You shall have no other gods before me." Settling this issue in your heart will produce the following in your home:

1. *It will simplify your authority.* It would be difficult for us to imagine just how unique and difficult it was for the nations in Moses' day to grasp the concept of "one God." Since their gods were mere figments of the imagination, they existed in abundance. And the number was growing! The existence of all these "gods" created enormous complications. Each was in charge of specific areas of life and had to be appealed to in the appropriate fashion. And to top it off, their gods didn't get along well among themselves. Appeasing one might get you in deep trouble with another. Altars were everywhere, and sacrifices ran the gamut from hares to humans.

Abraham arrived at Canaan, the crossroads of the world, with the message that there was just one God. He further complicated the issue by insisting that the way to God was by faith rather than works. That message kept him and his descendants in constant conflict with their neighbors, producing tensions that ultimately led to an extended period of slavery in Egypt. When God provided deliverance under the leadership of Moses, they once again set their faces toward the Promised Land. But on their journey homeward, God made it perfectly clear that He alone was to be in charge. This is the message Moses brought back from Mt. Sinai: "You shall have no other gods before [in addition to] Me." This first commandment, as with all of God's commandments, was to be clearly established and communicated through the institution of the family.

Hear, O Israel: The LORD our God, the LORD is one!
You shall love the LORD your God with all your heart,
with all your soul, and with all your might. And these
words which I command you today shall be in your heart;
you shall teach them diligently to your children, and shall
talk of them when you sit in your house, when you walk
by the way, when you lie down, and when you rise up.
(Deut. 6:4–7)

In fact, Israel's prosperity in the land of promise was directly tied to the effectiveness with which these principles were embraced and taught to succeeding generations. God stated that compliance with them was essential so ". . . that it may be well with you, and that you may multiply greatly" (Deut. 6:1–3).

When it is clearly established in your home that God is the Ultimate Authority and that His Word is the revelation of His will, issues that seem complicated and difficult to resolve are immediately simplified and settled. Finding direction and making decisions for your life and family become a matter of seeking His will as revealed by His Spirit through His Word. Instead of confusion and delay, there will be clarity and decisiveness.

When it is clearly established in your home that God is the Ultimate Authority, the exercise of godly discipline replaces mere outbursts of punishment. Discipline communicates value and a sense of future possibility. It is measured out with the knowledge that God is both the audience and the One to whom a parent must give an account. It must, therefore, be approached in the same manner that God disciplines His children, with both resolute determination and a full measure of grace.

When it is clearly established in your home that God is the Ultimate Authority, respect for others, especially those in positions of authority, is seen as a matter directly impacting an individual's relationship with God. Refusing to honor a parent, for instance, is also refusing to honor God. From His Word we discover the importance of obedience and right-hearted submission to authority as well as the dangers inherent in rebellion and self-centered resistance.

2. *It will settle your affections.* A once-popular song expressed
the struggles associated with being "torn between two lovers."
I suppose the song's popularity waned because now it is common
to become torn between more than two lovers. Once young married couples looked forward to buying a "starter house." Now
"starter marriages" are recommended as the proper introduction to
family life. The idea behind this is that you learn what you can in
your first marriage, then settle down for the real thing once you've
gotten the hang of it! This kind of thinking goes out the window
when you establish God in the position of Ultimate Authority. That
simple choice will settle the *affection question* once and for all. God
says, "I am to be the first and foremost recipient of your devotion.
After that, I will see to it that the others I bring into your life
receive the love and devotion they both need and deserve."

God's claim for first place in our hearts is justified. "After all,"
He says, "I am the LORD your God, who brought you out of . . .
bondage" (Exod. 20:2). In other words, He should be first in our
heart by reason of His devotion *to* us and His deliverance *of* us. No
wonder He refuses any other gods the privilege of receiving the
slightest nod of affection from us!

Those in God's Kingdom Family understand that when we put
God first in our devotion, He makes of us channels through which
the proper kind of love, His love, is poured out to others. When
I stand facing a young couple at the marriage altar, I remind them
that there is no safer place for them in the heart of their husband
or wife than second place, provided the Lord is in first place. God
will see to our partner's need *if* He is allowed the place of Ultimate
Authority in our heart.

Some years ago I visited with a man whose concern was that his
wife was rejecting his overtures of affection. "She's always too
tired," he sighed, "or she has a headache or too much to do or
too much on her mind at the moment. I don't know what the problem is," he continued, "and I surely don't know how to solve it."
I could tell he was even wondering if he had married the right
woman.

I asked him if he was aware of the often-used analogy in the Scriptures, portraying our relationship with Christ as that of His bride (the church), with Him (Christ) as the groom. He assured me that he understood this analogy, so I proceeded with this question: "How many times recently has Christ, your Lord, made an overture of affection to you, only to hear that you have a headache, you're too tired, or you're too busy and distracted?" He admitted that his own devotional life was in shambles. For weeks he had neglected the practice of prayer and Bible reading. "Interestingly," he said, "I have offered the same line to God that I have heard from my wife—too busy, tired, and distracted."

He got the picture! Later when I visited with him, he acknowledged that both his devotional life and his relationship with his wife had drastically improved. "Ironically," he said, "I never mentioned another word to my wife about our problems. I just corrected my relationship with the Lord. He is the One who has made all the difference!"

I never cease to be amazed at how a proper grasp of the principle of God as "Ultimate Authority" invades so many areas of our lives and establishes order, balance, and a sense of priority. When He is the recipient of our first love and devotion, we will not be torn between two, three, or more lovers. He settles our affections.

3. *It will screen your associations.* This "One God" issue separated Israel from all of her neighbors, not to mention all the others on the face of God's earth. It became the plumb line, or standard, by which their earthly relationships were judged. This standard was to be applied to their marriages, their families, their relationships with other nations—everything! It was an allegiance that both divided people from them and drew people to them. It will do the same for you and every member of God's Kingdom Family.

It is true that our allegiance to God can become a *dividing* issue. Relationships are always put to the test when it becomes evident that a person possesses an unwavering faith in the Lord. Israel's history records the truth of that statement. When reentering Canaan, for instance, with Joshua as leader, God reminded

Israel that under no circumstances was she to make any alliance (or treaties) with the people currently occupying the land. Throughout her history, God's judgment has fallen on Israel every time she has ignored this principle and adopted the worship and practices of other nations.

Have you ever "taken heat" because you are a believer in Christ? If you are a true believer, you probably have. There is a contemporary "push" among some Christians—both individuals and groups—emphasizing the importance of being like everyone else or identifying with them. They say that Christ left heaven and became as we are so that He might die for us. It's possible they have forgotten that He also "was in all points tempted as we are, yet without sin" (Heb. 4:15).

Jesus was in the world yet not of the world, and He commands His Kingdom Family members to live in the same fashion (2 Cor. 6:14–17). If He had not possessed convictions that were different from those around Him, they would not have crucified Him. This is not a call to prudishness or a holier-than-thou attitude, nor is it a call to be weird. It *is* a call to be different.

Shortly after Israel returned to Canaan, there was a remarkable occurrence that vividly illustrated how a faith that adheres to God's authority will effectively screen our associations. After the fall of Jericho, Israel went up against the comparatively small neighboring city of Ai. With Jericho behind them, Ai should have been a cakewalk. But Israel was met with astounding defeat! The defeat occurred because *one man* named Achan refused to obey God and hid plunder from Jericho (Exod. 6–7). God instructed Israel not to proceed until this one man was sought out, judged, and sentenced to death along with his family. This was no time for compromise!

Here is the point: Your faith will make a difference in your friendships.

But, there is another dynamic at work in God's Kingdom Families. Their lives of singular and selfless devotion to the Lord literally *draw* others into the circle of His grace. The intensity of their love for the Lord will be translated into love for their neighbor. Even those who might not initially appear to appreciate their devotion to God, often come first to respect it, then ultimately to seek it for themselves.

In the days that followed, "great fear came upon all the church" (v. 11) and on the other "believers were more increasingly added to the Lord, multitudes of both men and women." There you have a picture of both the dividing and the drawing power that is present when God's people worship Him and Him alone.

When Fidel Castro's communist regime first gained power in Cuba, many Christian missionaries were arrested and incarcerated. That's the "dividing" that sometimes takes place when a person loves God above all. But I was later privileged to hear firsthand how unbelieving prisoners and guards alike were drawn to Christ by witnessing the love those same Christian prisoners had for God and for them as well. That's the drawing power of an intense love for the Lord.

4. It will specify your ambitions. Kingdom Family members who seek to love God above all and to express that love through simple obedience to Him will discover an almost immediate impact on their ambitions. Love and devotion to God will change their behavior and their goals.

One of my longtime friends was a nightclub owner and professional gambler. When he came to Christ his ambitions radically changed. His live-in girlfriend, a dancer in his clubs, also came to know Christ just days afterward. I had the priviledge of performing their marriage. Now they have a God-honoring family, faithful in their service to Him. He has answered God's call to the ministry, completed his seminary education, and is serving faithfully on a church staff. When God becomes the Ultimate Authority in our lives, He changes our ambitions!

The minister to children in our church first came to us while trying to kick an addiction to smoking and drinking. Now, having met Christ and choosing to serve Him above all, he is a college graduate, married and the father of five beautiful children, and a minister to hundreds of children and their families. His life shows how reverence for God changes an individual's desires and focus.

One week, long before time for our midweek prayer service, I greeted a friend whom I had the privilege of leading to Christ over the telephone almost two years ago. Over the years his drinking had brought him virtually to the point of despair and death. Now, still sober and with a decent job, he was at church early because he "didn't want to miss anything!" He has a new hunger in life.

Last week I visited with a friend whom I first met when he appeared at the door of my office. Our students had led him to Christ in the restaurant where he worked and told him to come to our church if he wanted to grow. This former short-order cook is now a seminary graduate, minister, and counselor. Changed ambitions!

This past year an evangelist stood to give a report in our church. As he spoke, I could not help thinking of the night he trusted Christ in a church I was pastoring. Since that time, this former gang member with a rap sheet as long as your arm has served as a missionary in Africa and now ministers in prisons and high schools across the United States. When God is running the show, your focus in life changes remarkably!

Here is the point: Loving the Lord above all will change your life and give focus to your ambitions. It will make a difference in you and in your family. It not only changes how you think, but it also changes what you do. Jesus said, "If you love Me, *keep My commandments*" (John 14:15, emphasis mine).

HONORING GOD'S AUTHORITY

I sat listening as a man, caught in immorality and unfaithfulness, spilled out what was obviously a carefully crafted confession. There was no remorse, no tears, and no real desire to be reconciled with his wife. It was obvious that he had made some critical choices and did not intend to turn back. Visiting with the pastor was just a polite formality, a means of accommodating his wife's desperate attempt to put the marriage back together. It was his final words that grabbed me somewhere deep inside and provoked a visceral reaction that shocked us both.

"I know what you're thinking, preacher," he said with a nervous grin. "You're thinking I'm probably not a Christian and that I don't love the Lord. But you see, I really do love the Lord with all my heart. I guess I'm like King David."

"No, you don't love the Lord with all your heart," I replied and in a tone so loud it surprised us both. "And you're not like King David who melted when confronted by the prophet of God! Time will tell if you're a Christian because if you are He will treat you like one of His kids who deserves discipline. But one thing is certain, you don't love the Lord."

"You see," I continued, "if you love the Lord, you will do what He says. But what you are saying is that you do not intend to do what He says. You are determined to leave your wife and family and live in an immoral relationship. Say what you will, but you do not love the Lord."

When you have come to grips with what it means to love God above all—to have no other gods before Him—your entire approach to life is affected. Consider Joseph who, under some serious temptation by Potiphar's wife, said, "How then can I do this great wickedness, and sin against God?" (Gen. 39:9). While conscious of his position and of his master's trust, his main concern was what this behavior would do to his relationship with a holy God whom he loved, trusted, and served.

"What would Jesus do?" That was the question upon which Charles Sheldon's classic book *In His Steps* was based. The contemporary equivalent can be found in the WWJD bracelets worn by many believers. As a Kingdom Family member you will consider the manner in which your life will be spent, asking a similar question: Is this the direction that most pleases the Lord? Will you honor God's authority?

Dwight L. Moody, evangelist, author, and founder of the great Moody Bible Institute, said that he once overheard a simple statement that set the course for his life. The statement? "The world has yet to see what God could do with the life of a man totally committed to Him." To which Moody replied in his heart, "I will be that man." From that moment on, he determined that his life would be an example of the lordship of Christ.

It is a little wonder that God's initial commandment was stated in such a powerful form, a negative, in fact. "You shall have no other gods before Me" (Exod. 20:3). It is only when that principle is established in your thinking, embraced in your heart, and endorsed by your behavior that you can fully enjoy what it means to be part of God's Kingdom Family.

Thinking It Through, Living It Out

1. Do you consciously live each day "as unto the Lord," or under His authority? Is there a time in your prayer life each day when you deliberately surrender to His will? Do you believe He is your Sovereign by virtue of both creation and redemption?

2. Do those around you have some idea of your allegiance to the Lord? How would they classify your brand of Christian living? Hot? Cold? Lukewarm? Bold? Fearful? Consistent? Sensitive? Would they be surprised to hear you say that you believe in God and have come to Him by faith in Jesus Christ?

3. Are you conscious of any area of your life in which you are, by your willful disobedience, now saying to God, "I don't love You"? If so, what do you intend to do about that area of rebellion to His authority in your life? Are there people in your family from whom you need to seek forgiveness for rebelling against their authority?

4. Does the respect you have for God have an effect on your relationships with others, especially those in positions of authority? Do you believe God is at work through systems of authority such as in government or in the home? Can you think of examples of God's will being carried out even by those who do not reverence Him?

5. "Honoring God's authority" is the first of *The Seven Pillars of a Kingdom Family*. Will you read through the statement at the beginning of the chapter? Will you "sign on" by establishing this principle in your thinking, embracing it with your heart, and endorsing it by your behavior?

Human life is a gift from God and is of transcendent worth. It is to be treasured, protected, encouraged, and loved from the moment of conception until the moment of death. I know that each member of my family must ultimately give an account to God, and forgiveness of sin and eternal life in heaven require personal repentance of sin and faith in Christ. I will honor God by expressing self-sacrificial love to each of my family members throughout the entirety of their lives (Eph. 20:13; Ps. 119:13–16, 127–128; Prov. 16:31).

Chapter Three

RESPECTING HUMAN LIFE

I met the couple in the hallway of the hospital where I had been visiting with the husband's ailing mother. As we visited briefly, he expressed a concern I have heard on many similar occasions. "Pastor, what do you think we should do with my mother?"

I am often asked this question, and I normally respond with the assurance of prayer as they sort through the decisions facing them. But on this occasion I was startled not so much by its substance as by the manner and tone in which it was asked. He could well have been asking, "What do you think we should do with our old refrigerator? It doesn't work well, and it's in the way. You know, more of a nuisance than anything else. Got any good ideas? Can't just throw it away. At least, I'd rather not, anyway."

Admittedly, his was a dilemma with which many in our society are struggling. Longer, more healthy living, coupled with the astounding capabilities of modern medicine, have brought our society into uncharted territory. The term *sandwich generation* has been coined to refer to the growing group of individuals who are simultaneously confronted with the responsibilities of rearing children, and sometimes grandchildren, while also tending to the growing needs of aging parents. What is the answer?

This is not the only problem confronting our society. Many other people are considering options for an unwanted pregnancy, something they see as an unnecessary complication. Citing "women's rights" and "freedom of choice," they are in full support of the booming business of abortion. Unfortunately, they most often fail to realize fully the downside to this gruesome practice, with the result that there are growing numbers of disillusioned, guilt-ridden, emotionally spent mothers who never allowed their child to see the light of day. Add to that an equally large number of fathers who are moving on with life as they please, a life devoid of any sense of personal responsibility for their actions.

Still another issue is beginning to dominate the news (which, by the way, reports only the tip of this iceberg). Having decided that the unborn are dispensable and wondering if the aged should be disposable, the ultimate conclusion is that no one, at any age, should interfere with our good times. Now the practice of child abuse, child molestation, and pornography are at all-time highs. In the minds of many, life at every age has lost its value. Other individuals are considered essential only as long as they serve the ultimate goals of the good life.

Against this dismal and perplexing backdrop, members of God's Kingdom Family assert that all human life (at whatever age, or in whatever emotional or physical condition) is a gift from God and of transcendent worth, deserving of self-sacrificial love throughout the entirety of their lives. Kingdom Family members are committed to honoring God by respecting human life.

But how does this play out in terms of the choices we must make every day, choices that impact how we respond to our family members, however old or indisposed? How can you give each member of your family, young or old, the attention, love, and respect God says they deserve? What do we do about the out-of-wedlock pregnancy? How can we respond properly to a parent whose physical (and perhaps mental) condition is fragile and in need of almost constant care? What principles should guide our thinking so that we handle life at any age or stage with the respect and love it deserves?

GOD VALUES YOUR LIFE . . . INFINITELY

"Human life is a gift from God and is of transcendent worth" begins this section of the Kingdom Family commitment. This is an affirmation that flies in the face of much contemporary thinking. Yet it is true! Listen to the words of the psalmist:

> For *You* [God] formed my inward parts;
> You wove me in my mother's womb.
> I will give thanks to *You*, for I am fearfully and
> wonderfully made;
> Wonderful are *Your* works,
> And my soul knows it very well.
> My frame was not hidden from *You*,
> When I was made in secret,
> And skillfully wrought in the depths of the earth;
> *Your* eyes have seen my unformed substance;
> And in *Your* book they were all written
> The days that were ordained for me,
> When as yet there was not one of them.
> (Ps. 139:13–16 NASB, emphasis mine)

Not only is God sovereignly involved in each person's conception, but He also has a specific role for each life to fulfill. Listen to the prophet, Jeremiah: Now the word of the LORD came to me say-ing, "Before I *formed* you in the womb I *knew* you, and before you were born I *consecrated* you; I *have appointed* you a prophet to the nations" (Jer. 1:4–5 NASB, emphasis mine).

The apostle Paul shared a similar understanding by noting that God "set me apart even from my mother's womb, and called me through His grace" (Gal. 1:15).

Human life is a gift from God and is of transcendent worth. It must be treated as such regardless of one's age or physical condi-tion. To do anything less is to assume a role God has reserved for Himself as Creator of life. There is no point at which any human life is more or less important to God, nor should there be to us.

GOD KNOWS YOU . . . INTIMATELY

God knows you perfectly and desires your best. Securing what seems best for you, however, does not require the sacrifice of what is best for another. He has that individual's welfare in mind as well. David reflected on God's perfect knowledge of us and wrote:

> O LORD, you have searched me and known me.
> You know when I sit down and when I rise up;
> You understand my thought from afar.
> You scrutinize my path and my lying down,
> And are intimately acquainted with all my ways.
> (Ps. 139:1–3 NASB)

When confronted with hard choices regarding the welfare of a family member, it is imperative to stop, take a deep breath, and prayerfully remind yourself that God has a plan for this person's future as well as yours. Your responsibility is simply to seek His plan and then act in concert with it. By responding to others as God leads, you are acting in concert with His plan for your life as well. This makes your response incredibly important. And, if you think about it, this approach can be remarkably liberating. You are set free to do the very thing God created you to do!

While in college I had the privilege of conducting a revival in a small town in southern Arkansas. Prior to the service one evening, the revival team was invited to eat in the home of a faithful church member. I have rarely met such a gracious and genuinely contented woman. Throughout the meal I was impressed with her joyful attitude and spiritual depth.

After the meal, this lady said, "I'd like to show you a living illustration of God's love." We had no idea anyone else was in this home, so we prepared to go outdoors. She indicated that this "living illustration" was in a bedroom in the back of the house, so we followed her there. Imagine our surprise when we were led into a room where a grown man was lying in something similar to a baby's bed. He could not communicate with us and, in fact, was unable to do the slightest thing for himself.

As we gazed, speechless, that lady said, "This is my son. He was born and has lived his entire life in this condition. I must tend to every need he has. As you can see, he doesn't have the ability to communicate, so he can never tell me what he needs, nor can he express gratitude to me."

As her words and the child's plight began to sink in, she continued, "Many people encouraged me to place him in a state home for children like him. I don't feel bad toward those who do. I have met some of those parents and feel that they made the best decision for them. But as I prayed, God showed me that He wanted me to keep my son here in my home. Have I questioned God about this? Certainly! Especially after my husband died. But I must tell you that tending to his needs has been the greatest joy of my life. It has taught me to depend on God as never before. The doctors say that soon my son may die. I'll have no regrets, not even for one minute of the time I've spent with him. And one day in heaven, we will walk and talk together about all we *both* experienced during these many wonderful days together."

I have heard similar testimonies from friends who have for years tended to the needs of an ailing spouse, child, or parent. Sometimes, because of the special demands of their situation, they have been in care centers; other times they have been in the home. But the most glowing testimonies come from those who realize as someone said, "Life is not just about me, my joy, my success, my happiness. It is about all of us and the plan God has for our lives!" God knows what's best for each of us individually and all of us together. Our responsibility is to find God's plan, then lovingly and graciously commit ourselves to it.

GOD CARES FOR YOU . . . INTENSELY

A great deal is being said and written these days about those who are in the later years of life and the choices facing them and their family members. It has become far too easy for those who are emotionally detached from a situation simply to decide that an individual must not be capable of enjoying the proper quality of life. The nagging concern in the minds of many senior adults, for instance, is expressed in the question, What will happen to me? And many confess to the silent fear of being trundled off to a facility designed more for their death than their life. They know how easy it is for those who are out of sight soon to be out of mind.

Kingdom Family members know that God has the answer for this time in life as well. Whatever the answer, it will be consistent with the persistent care God provides for His children. David's psalm continues to be instructive:

> Where can I go from Your Spirit?
> Or where can I flee from Your presence?
> If I ascend to heaven, You are there;
> If I make my bed in Sheol, behold, You are there.
> If I take the wings of the dawn,
> If I dwell in the remotest part of the sea,
> Even there Your hand will lead me,
> And Your right hand will lay hold of me.
> If I say, "Surely the darkness will overwhelm me,
> And the light around me will be night,"
> Even the darkness is not dark to You,

And the night is as bright as day.

Darkness and light are alike to You.

(Ps. 139:7–12 NASB)

The bottom line for David was the omnipresence of God. He is present wherever we are—caring, loving, sacrificing.

I have been taken by the thought that, by God's grace, an individual's utility, or usefulness, increases with age right up to the moment God calls us home. Some of the greatest sermons ever preached, and some of the greatest responses ever recorded, have been delivered by the Spirit of God to family members gathered at the bedside of a dying relative.

My own mother lay comatose in a hospital bed for several weeks before her death. Each of her children has since shared that at some point, when alone with her in that bedside vigil, they made some significant decisions in light of her imminent death— decisions motivated by her love for us and the strength of her character. Her utility for God increased right up to the moment of her death.

If usefulness to God is sustained until the moment of our death, then we should care for our family members with that in view. In our church are a number of families who have children with serious impairments to otherwise normal development. (As a matter of fact, we have a ministry to our local Cerebral Palsy Center.) I never cease to be amazed at the spiritual impact of these family members on their caregivers. One husband and wife, for example, have adopted and are rearing their own granddaughter who has disabilities because of a parent's drug use. Severely impaired at birth and neglected by her own mother, this young girl was destined to spend the balance of her life in an institution. But she was rescued by her grandparents and has, by their testimony, contributed more to them than they ever imagined contributing to her.

Another couple cares for their own daughter who, injured at birth, is a quadriplegic. In addition to never walking, talking, or eating without assistance, she has impaired hearing and sight and can perform literally no function on her own. She has her own room at home, a room that is clean, bright, and cheery. She is adored by her parents, her two brothers, and her two sisters. She goes everywhere they go and has, in fact, been a bridesmaid in three of her siblings' weddings. (I have performed all three. Two of the children in fact are married to two of ours!) They cannot imagine life without her!

Recently I visited in the home of one of our senior adult couples as they celebrated their sixtieth wedding anniversary. The house was packed with loving church and family members. Long ago some might have suggested that the bride of sixty years should be placed in a care center. That day might rightly come, in fact. And if it does, the family will proceed with love, attentiveness, care, and dignity. But for now the husband and family just "love taking care of Mom." Her husband said to me with tears one day, "I'm enjoying fulfilling this part of my marriage vow."

These people are my heroes and heroines. I want to be like them. Instead of thinking of their own life's little comforts, they have given themselves to caring for other family members at crucial times in their lives. In the end they will discover that in the process they were fulfilling God's great design for their lives as well. They were becoming like their Master.

IMPLICATIONS

Having grasped the significance of the infinite value God places on your life and all human life, His intimate knowledge of us, and His intense concern for our welfare, we should think seriously about the manner in which we, as members of His Kingdom Family, respond to our own family members in the various stages of life's pilgrimage. Several principles should serve as guides to our thinking. I call these the principles of interest, initiation, and inspiration.

1. Interest—If God values us infinitely, we should, at the very least, communicate to each of our family members just how much we value them and our relationship with them. This occurs when we express our genuine interest in them.

Remarkably, some people simply do not possess a genuine interest in the welfare of their family members. I remember speaking with such a man on a flight one evening. In the quietness disturbed only by the whispered rush of air as the miles passed below us, I asked if he was headed home. His affirmative reply opened the door for a discussion about our families. In a moment of unusual candidness, he said, "I have no idea where my son is these days, and frankly I don't care." Then he told me how in an explosive moment of anger they had parted ways. "I suppose he'll call me if he needs me," sighed the man, "but that may never happen." What he didn't realize was that he needed his son more than he would ever know or admit. And his son needed him!

We all need others who really care about our welfare. God has a passionate interest in our welfare. In the parable of the prodigal son, it is instructive to see how the father sees his son at a distance and runs to meet him. Later the same caring father goes out to talk with the pouting elder brother. In both instances you cannot miss the point: God cares. And we should care desperately about the welfare of our family members—even if, as in the case of the prodigal, we are hard-pressed to respond in a fashion that makes sense to others.

Our interest in the welfare of others should be prompted by God's interest in us. Here again, David's psalm is revealing:

> How precious also are Your thoughts to me, O God!
> How great is the sum of them!
> If I should count them, they would be more in number than the sand;
> When I awake, I am still with You.
> (Ps. 139:17–18)

People have a way of knowing who is genuinely interested in their welfare. Which one of us has not seen the football player on the sidelines, grinning into the camera and mouthing, "Hi, Mom!" Yes, Dad may have attended all those games, played catch until dark, and coached Little League after coming home dog tired from work. But in the heat of the moment, the field-warrior sheds his macho image long enough to greet the most caring person he knows, the one person he knows is interested in his welfare, even if she doesn't understand the game.

Have you communicated genuine interest to each of your family members? Do you know the real spiritual condition of each one? This is not something you can accomplish by simply saying you are interested in them and their welfare. Communicating your interest takes self-sacrificing love, time, energy, questions, prayer, and follow-up.

In one chapter of our book *Letters to Lovers,* my wife, Jeannie, and I deal with the "in-law issue." We note the incredible qualities possessed by Moses' father-in-law, Jethro, qualities every in-law should seek to emulate. Right up there at the head of the list is "genuine interest." Jethro came to see Moses, went to work with him, asked questions, and then made suggestions with the caveat, "if the Lord is pleased to bless this." Even after returning home, Moses was so impressed with Jethro's interest in his welfare that it remains recorded in the Pentateuch.

2. *Initiation*—God knows us intimately. That being the case, you should initiate activities that communicate your desire to know the "heart" of your family members on such crucial issues as life and death. If you have not had a discussion with your family members regarding your desire to do the right thing at every juncture of life, you should initiate one now, regardless of who you are. Don't wait for others to bring up the subject. Many great discussions have never taken place simply because someone was waiting on another to bring up the issue.

The apostle Paul initiated such a discussion by writing openly of his concerns. "I'm in a bind," he writes in the first chapter of Philippians, "having a desire to die and be with Christ, which would be best. But right now it's more necessary for me to stick around and help you. So that's what I will do. I will stay, spend time with you, and help you grow and rejoice in your faith" (Phil. 1:23–25, author's paraphrase).

Paul was opening a discussion on a subject that was probably on the minds of many who refused to discuss it for "propriety's sake." You need to do the same. Be wise. Pick the appropriate venue and time. Express your love for your family and then ask, "Could we talk about something that will one day face each of us? How should we respond to one another? What are your desires? What do you think would be the response that most honors God's heart?"

Get prepared for both tears and smiles. This will be a tender moment and one that you will probably not care to repeat often. Of course, there will most likely be some humor as well. Recently, an ailing family matriarch turned to me in the presence of her children and grandchildren and said, "Pastor, when I die, I'd like to be stuffed and mounted over the kitchen table. That way they'll know I'm still watching what they eat and listening to what they say!" Her humor took the edge off what she knew was a difficult moment for her children. It was another way of communicating her concern for them!

3. *Inspiration*—God is intensely concerned for your welfare. His concern, in fact, was ultimately illustrated by sending His Son who ultimately gave His life for us. Writing of this event, the apostle Paul said:

> Let this mind be in you, which was also in Christ Jesus: Who, being in the form of God, thought it not robbery to be equal with God: But made himself of no reputation, and took upon him the form of a servant, and was made in the likeness of men: and being found in fashion as a man, he humbled himself, and became obedient unto death, even the death of the cross. Wherefore God also hath highly exalted him, and given him a name which is above every name: That at the name of Jesus every knee should bow, of things in heaven, and things in earth, and things under the earth; and that every tongue should confess that Jesus Christ is Lord, to the glory of God the Father. (Phil. 2:5–11 KJV)

"Jesus," wrote Paul, "is to be your inspiration, your model, your example. Let His mind be in you!"

Your concern for your family is a model for those who follow
you. Your attentiveness, sensitivity, and faithfulness inspire them to
follow your example. As a friend of mine says, "I know that by the
way I am tending to the needs of my parents, I am teaching my
children how to care for theirs!"

Using the biblical reference from Galatians 6:7 (often called
the Law of the Harvest), those of us in Oklahoma say, "What goes
'round, comes 'round." I saw this law vividly illustrated one summer in, of all places, a worn-down nursing home in a small
Oklahoma town. I think you'll get the picture *and* the principle.

I had traveled to the town with a friend who had business
there. Since we needed to visit about another issue, I had offered
to come along for the ride. After he had completed his task, he
asked if I would mind doing just one more thing before returning
home.

"There's a nursing home out here at the edge of town," he said.
"When I lived here, I used to conduct Bible studies on Sunday
afternoons. It was there I met Miss Pansy."

Over the next few minutes he described Miss Pansy as a leg-
end in that small town. An African-American, she had woven her
way into the heart of virtually every family in town, white or black.
Her constant, loving care coupled with her desire to stay "out of the
picture" had brought her to a position of quiet influence in a pre-
dominantly white community. Whenever a family faced a need,
somehow Miss Pansy was there to minister to them. When a death
occurred, she would quietly knock on the back door and invite herself in to clean the house. If someone was suffering from an illness,
she would leave a jar of her famous vegetable soup on the back
steps. If someone was out of town, she'd weed the garden or feed
the pets.

But now Miss Pansy was in a nursing home, and my friend
didn't feel he could leave town without stopping by to see what she
might need. We parked the car out front, greeted several weary
oldsters, and made our way into the darkened hallways of the
home.

"Miss Pansy?" said my friend, knocking on her door. When there was no answer, he gently pushed open the door. Through the small opening I saw a stooped figure in a wheelchair, facing the wall, hands folded in prayer. "Miss Pansy?" my friend said again, only louder.

At his last greeting, Miss Pansy turned her chair around, revealing her kind, wizened countenance and beautiful, snow-white hair. A smile broke across here face. "Why," she said, "Brother John! I was just telling the Lord I had need of seeing you. Lo and behold, here you are. Isn't the Lord so good!"

Miss Pansy was reaping in her last days the same kind of sensitive care and attention she had sown all her life. She had inspired others with the example of her life. Now she was reaping the benefit of that inspiration. It occurred to me that, elsewhere in that nursing home, there were probably people with hardened faces set toward the wall, cursing uncaring children and friends who never called. In truth, they really had no cause for complaint. You see, they, too, were reaping what they had sown—the neglect, the indifference, the unfaithfulness of many years.

KNOW MY HEART!

The whole issue of life's transcendent value and our need to care for our family members throughout the entirety of their lives gives us reason to ask some serious questions about our relationship with them. David approached this investigation even more seriously. He asked God to do the searching: "Search me, O God, and know my heart: try me, and know my thoughts: And see if there be any wicked way in me, and lead me in the way everlasting" (Ps. 139:23–24 KJV).

Why is he so concerned that the Lord perform this search of his heart? Why should we, as members of His Kingdom Family, feel the same? I think it is because of what he has already discovered and expressed so eloquently. God values human life infinitely; He knows each one of us intimately; He cares for us all intensely.

Who better to show us the truth about ourselves? And who
else could give us grace to change and lead us in the way
everlasting?

Thinking It Through, Living It Out

1. As you consider your responsibilities to your own family, are
   there any that are, or will soon be, difficult to resolve? Do
   these involve the actual physical welfare of a family member (aging, physical disabilities, etc.)? Are you the one primarily assigned the responsibility of resolving the issue?
   Does your family resolve situations like this as a team?

2. Have you and the other members of your family, come to
   the basic conclusions about the transcendent value of
   human life as expressed in the Kingdom Family
   Commitment? Are there past decisions that did not reflect
   this thinking? Have you, or those involved, repented and
   sought forgiveness so that you might move ahead with God's
   blessing?

3. Do you believe God has the answer for the decision facing
   you? Are you committed to finding His answer and acting
   in concert with it? Are you willing to initiate the discussion
   regarding the hard choices you might face in the future?
   Are you determined to resolve them in a manner that will
   both assure the welfare of all involved and bring honor to
   God?

4. What "legacy of concern" are you passing along to others in
   your family? Do they think of you as a caring individual or
   as someone who doesn't want to be troubled with others'
   problems? How are you currently communicating your concern for each of the other members of your family?

5. Are you working to bring together the various members of your family in a manner that spans the barriers of age, mobility, interest, etc.? Are the youngest members of your family aware of their heritage? Do the senior adults in your family feel that their involvement is desired and valued? Do the children in your family hold parents and grandparents in high respect? Do the adults in your family show proper interest in the children?

God has established the family as His first institution on earth. It is worthy of my most noble aspirations and commitments, including my commitment to moral purity, marital fidelity, and Christlike love for each family member. Because marriage is a picture of Christ's faithfulness to His bride, the church, and because the family is a picture of the Father's faithfulness to His children, I will honor the Lord by being faithful and pure (Exod. 20:14; 1 Cor. 6:18–19; Job 31:1; Matt. 5:27–30).

CHAPTER FOUR

EXERCISING MORAL PURITY

W̲e live in a society that has mastered the art of compartmentalization. Many people familiar with church life are also familiar with the term "Sunday Christians." This term has been used over the years to describe those whose attendance in worship on Sunday is not matched by an equally faithful exercise of Christian character or discipline throughout the other six days of the week. In reality, that's more characteristic of the kind of compartmentalizing that took place in days gone by. Things have changed!

Today some worshipers are comfortable being in church on Sunday morning, hands held high in praise and a rapturous eyes-closed smile on their face, and being in bed with their "lover" on

Sunday evening. By the way, the lover to whom I am referring is not their husband or wife but someone with whom they have established an out-of-wedlock relationship. This is a newer, higher form of compartmentalization, an ability to isolate, or segment, one moment from another, an ability to demand certain moral standards in one arena and reject them outright in another.

THE SESAME STREET GENERATION

I have often referred to this as the Sesame Street Generation. Think about it for a moment. Most of us are familiar with this enormously popular Public Television children's program loaded with interesting characters, both real and make-believe. *Sesame Street* is deliberately designed to hold a child's attention over a sustained period of time. Program segments are often field-tested for best results before airing. In rapid succession, scenes, characters, and focus change from one segment to the next. One moment the emphasis is on a specific color, the next a number, then a puppet vignette with a song, followed by larger-than-life characters who interact with normal-sized people.

Sesame Street's success depends on the viewer's ability to compartmentalize, to isolate, the events and emotions of one moment from the next. The success of this program is legendary as evidenced by many attempts to duplicate its format. But while both interesting and highly educational, the downside to the program is the subtle manner in which it trains its viewers to compartmentalize other areas of life. There is, for instance, the highly respected businessman with the model family who has another side to his life, a secret and immoral relationship he has maintained for years; the housewife who is addicted to Internet romance, carrying on cyberchat with an unseen lover to whom she tells all; the pastor or church leader whose television or computer now takes him, unnoticed by others, into secret dens of sensuality; the student who is active in the youth program at church and, unknown to his or her parents, sexually active as well. Of course, we have joined the world in witnessing the ultimate debacle of compartmentalization: A national president who somehow saw no contradiction in being in church with his wife and daughter on Sunday morning and involved in an immoral relationship with another woman on Sunday afternoon.

Against this backdrop we have God's clarion call to specific moral standards that are to pervade every area of life: "You shall not commit adultery!" The stern nature of this command would also add, "Not here, not now, not anywhere, anytime, or under any circumstances!" Just to make certain we understood that His moral principles are to be both indelibly etched in our hearts and unfalteringly practiced in our lives, He precedes and follows that command with nine other nonoptional moral principles. Jesus later underscored them by saying in His Sermon on the Mount, "Don't even think about it!"

Members of God's Kingdom Family take seriously their Master's words. They know God has established the family as His first institution on earth. They believe it is worthy of their most noble aspirations and commitments, including their commitment to moral purity, marital fidelity, and Christlike love for each family member. Because marriage is a picture of Christ's faithfulness to His bride, the church, and because the family is a picture of the Father's faithfulness to His children, they have determined that, throughout the balance of their lives, they will honor the Lord by being faithful and pure.

But the question is, *how*? How can members of God's Kingdom Family establish and maintain lives characterized by a commitment to moral purity and marital fidelity? What steps can be taken to prevent the kind of moral lapses that devastate lives, dash hopes, and destroy families? How can a child of God become adequately armed to face the temptations seductively offered by Satan and win out over them? And how can an individual whose record is one of defeat and failure live out the balance of life in a manner that both pleases God and promotes integrity and trust?

YOUR HOME, A SACRED INSTITUTION

Throughout this book you will be reminded that God has established the home as a sacred institution. It is, in fact, God's first and, therefore, oldest institution on earth. Properly understood, it is to be where a person's spiritual pilgrimage begins and subsequently is formed. If you have not been blessed to be in a home where biblical principles are lived and taught, then you can—and should—ask God to enable you to be the first in line of a new generation of God-fearing and Christ-honoring people. After all, someone always must make such an initial choice if any home is to be founded on Christ. You should do all you can to protect and preserve holiness in your home. Your life should be a channel through which God brings blessing into your home. It should not be the means through which Satan enters into your family and ravages it.

The state of its marriages and families is the barometer by which any community should be measured. Moral impurity and the infidelity and adultery that accompany it are particularly devastating to the home. Such impurity creates an ever-widening circle of pain and heartache. And its impact is felt for generations to come! Recent studies, for instance, show that children growing up in single-parent families have a 300 percent greater chance of negative life impact than children growing up in homes with both parents present.

Until you understand God's heart regarding the family, it is doubtful that you will give much effort to avoiding those things that will destroy it. Often I have the sad duty of listening to the heart of a husband or wife who has been unfaithful as the consequences of their unfaithfulness are beginning to sink in. The people who love them the most have been lacerated and left behind as they gave way first to imagination, then temptation, and finally the realization of their fantasy. Now they cannot undo their sin. The pain, both theirs and their victims', is almost unbearable. "If I had only stopped to consider the wonderful gift God had given me with my family," they lament, often with tears coursing down their cheeks.

The family is more than God's first institution (Gen. 1:27–28; 2:24); it is a picture of our salvation (Eph. 5, especially v. 32). In the family we are to hear first about God and His ways (Deut. 6:7). From the father a child first receives a picture of the heavenly Father (Luke 11:13). Through the relationships of the home, the principles of authority and respect are communicated (Eph. 5:21; 6:1–3), as well as the importance of genuine love (Eph. 6:4). The moral principles regarding such issues as work, marriage, chastity, discipline, decisiveness, and benevolence are to be taught and modeled in the home (see the Book of Proverbs). In the home a child should most readily be able to hear and respond to the gospel (2 Tim. 1:5; Acts 10; 16:30–34).

Little wonder that God places such emphasis on the home! And little wonder that a high and biblical view of the home is an incredibly effective motivation to shun anything that might damage family relationships. Mess with the family and you will find your-self dealing one-on-one with God. Ask Isaac and his family about it (see Gen. 25:20–35:29)!

Your Holiness, a Solemn Injunction

In addition to what God has said about the sanctity of the home, He commands each member of His Kingdom Family to live a life of personal holiness (1 Pet. 1:15–16). Such a life is an absolute contradiction to everything our society now communicates as being normal, natural, and even healthy. As a matter of fact, unless you willingly endorse the sex-oriented, perverted appetites espoused by many—especially through the media—you are charged with deny-ing them their "rights." Or, worse yet, your criticisms of their deviant behavior—whether perversions of a homosexual lifestyle or perversions among heterosexuals—can be challenged in court as a "hate crime."

No doubt about it, God's Ten Commandments may still be on the walls of our nation's Supreme Court, but they run absolutely counter to the grain of contemporary society. God says, "Do not commit adultery! Don't put your holiness, your walk with Me, your marriage, or your purity up for grabs." Christ both amplified and clarified this commandment, indicating that it included any lewdness or unchaste thought, as well as action (Matt. 5:27–28): "You have heard that it was said to those of old, 'You shall not commit adultery.' But I say to you that whosoever looks at a woman to lust for her has committed adultery with her in his heart."

"In other words," Jesus is saying, "holiness springs from the heart. That's where the books are kept!" Our tendency is to think that we are holy and pure as long as we *appear* that way to others. That's not the case, according to Jesus: "But the Lord said to him, 'Now you Pharisees make the outside of the cup and dish clean, but your inward part is full of greed and wickedness'" (Luke 11:39).

Holiness springs from the heart! It must be within the heart, then, that we establish our intentions to be morally pure and maritally faithful, expressing Christlike love for each member of our family.

Your Heart, a Significant Intention

The declared purpose of this chapter is to move you toward both the commitment to and the practice of moral purity, marital faithfulness (if married, or intend one day to be married), and Christlike love for each member of your family. You should not wait until you have come to a moral crossroad before making this decision. You should arrive at times of testing—and there will be many—with your moral compass already set in the right direction.

If, in fact, you have somehow already made a shipwreck of your life with poor and sinful moral choices, confess your sin, repent, or turn from it, claiming forgiveness in Christ. Determine that you will serve Him with the balance of your life. This does not mean that the earthly consequences of your sin will suddenly disappear or that God will remove all consequences of previous mistakes. Israel's four hundred years in Egypt were necessitated by the sinful behavior of Jacob's sons, a behavior they learned by closely watching him *prior* to his life-changing meeting with God at Jabbok. While Moses was forgiven of the sin of striking the rock the second time, he still was prohibited from entering Canaan. I insert this thought here because many are under the impression that they can "sow wild oats" through the simple act of confession and escape the privilege of reaping them.

What you can do, however, is acknowledge your sin and repent of it. Turn to Christ in faith—for salvation, if that issue has yet to be settled in your life; for restored fellowship and usefulness, if you are already a member of God's Kingdom Family—and determine that you will, by God's grace, seek to do the following:

1. Fill your heart with the Word of God. God's Word is remarkable in its power! By filling your heart with His Word, you first experience a dynamic cleansing of your thoughts. "You are already clean because of the word which I have spoken to you," said Jesus to His disciples on the eve of His crucifixion (John 15:3). Positive thinking is not only a good practice but also one we are exhorted to follow (Phil. 4:8). Here Christ is speaking of more than mere positive thinking. He is saying that His Word actually cleans out and replaces the evil thoughts and intents that have lodged in our heart.

But God's Word does even more! It continues to give us guidance, protection, and renewed thinking: "Wherewithal shall a young man cleanse his way? by taking heed thereto according to thy Word. . . . Thy Word have I hid in mine heart, that I might not sin against thee. . . . Thy Word is a lamp unto my feet, and a light unto my path" (Ps. 119:9, 11, 105 KJV).

When Solomon (who ought to know!) said to his son, "Keep your heart with all diligence, for out of it spring the issues of life" (Prov. 4:23), he was pointing to a practical manner in which his son could live out the truths quoted in these psalms. "Guard your heart (your mind, will, emotions)! Be careful what you put into it, for it is from your heart that you establish the boundaries of your life!" What better resource for establishing your life's boundaries (and your goals!) than the pure Word of God!

2. *Flee anything that is intended to incite lust.* There is a vast difference between love and lust. Lust, a strong, unholy passion, is brought to the surface when we give way before temptation. Paul exhorted young Timothy to "flee youthful lusts!" knowing that they can quickly become so imbedded in our character that they guide behavior for the balance of life.

I saw this principle vividly portrayed several years ago when flying from one city to another. While waiting in the lounge area for the departure of our flight, I could not help but notice a seedy-looking, older man who clutched a brown sack tightly in his hand. I thought to myself, *That guy's got some booze in the sack. After we board the flight, he'll start hitting his own private bottle. How sad to see the toll his addiction has taken on his life—physically, spiritually and morally.*

After being seated on the plane, I noticed the same man sitting opposite but one row forward of me. I settled back to see how long it would before he hit the bottle. Imagine my surprise when, after furtively glancing around to see if anyone was watching, he pulled out, not a liquor bottle, but a slick, pornographic magazine! This old man's life had been burned up in his pursuit of youthful lust!

A friend of mine is fond of quoting from Proverbs when tempted to give way before inducements to evil thoughts and actions: "My son, if sinners entice you, do not consent" (Prov. 1:10)! Later in that same book, Solomon describes the foolish young man (Prov. 7:22), who passed through the street near the house of the harlot, then went to her house like an "ox goes to the slaughter." "Her house," he reminded his son, "is the way to slaughter." Today's paths to the house of the wicked scarcely require leaving your home. You can turn down the path of the wicked on your television or computer. But remember, "The ways of man are before the eyes of the LORD, and He ponders all his paths" (Prov. 5:21). That's a good thing to remember when incited toward lust of any kind.

3. *Fix your heart on God's plan for your life and marriage.* "My heart is fixed, O God, my heart is fixed," exclaimed David

(Ps. 57:7 KJV). This was his way of saying that, by previous preparation, he was focusing on God's plan and provision for His life. Later he writes of the good man who "shall not be afraid of evil tidings: his heart is fixed, trusting in the LORD" (Ps. 112:7 KJV).

When God first began speaking to my own heart regarding marriage, I prayed that He would give me some "word" of direction for my life. He responded with more than a word! In fact, He gave me the entire fifth chapter of Ephesians as a template for the relationship I should have with my future wife. There were negatives to be avoided and positives to be accepted. For me, that pattern became the standard that I would hold up as I considered a future mate. Soon I met Jeannie who, by conviction and character, fulfilled the description of Ephesians 5. God had graciously given me that passage so that I might fix my heart upon it, and Him, as I considered the possibility of marriage.

Someone has said, "If you don't know where you're going, any old path will get you there." Of course, therein lies the problem! God doesn't want us traveling "any old path." He has a divinely conceived plan for us, a plan He is willing to reveal to those willing to search it out. Once found, it becomes a pole star upon which you can fix the compass of your life. It will guide you in your marriage and family relationships as well as in your work.

When Sir Ernest Shackleton was guiding his small skiff across the world's most tortuous sea in a desperate attempt to rescue the crew of the *Endurance*, it was of utmost importance that he and the others with him got a proper fix for navigational purposes. They were headed toward a relatively small island. Miss it and their chances of survival were virtually nil, not to mention the possibility of returning to rescue the additional crew members. So important was this fix that they were willing to brave icy-cold seas, which often ran over thirty feet high, in order to obtain it. Was it foolish to seek a fix in those conditions? Absolutely not! For without it all would be lost. Nor is it foolish for you to fix your heart on God and His Word. Failure here could plunge you into the icy seas of immorality.

4. Find a trustworthy individual and become accountable. If married, this person will in all likelihood be your life's mate. But you must be willing to let him or her walk unimpeded through the recesses of your heart. Or you may choose a close friend who is willing to ask you the hard questions of life. "As iron sharpens iron, so a man sharpens the countenance of his friend" (Prov. 27:17).

When Jesus sent out the disciples on their "trial run" (see Luke 10), He sent them out "two by two." There was divine wisdom behind that plan. Each person needs someone else in life to hold him accountable. This, in fact, is one of the benefits of being actively involved in a church family where you can provoke one another unto love and good works (see Heb. 10:24).

Several years ago I read a book by Charles Blair entitled *The Man Who Could Do No Wrong.* The book chronicled a dismal period in the life of this widely acclaimed pastor in Denver, Colorado. In describing the events that led to the collapse of his ministerial empire, Blair observed that a fatal mistake was surrounding himself with men who were *complimentary* of him rather than *complementary* to him. There is a huge difference between the two. In the first instance, one finds men who were simply "rubber stamps" for his position on virtually anything. Telling him the sky was the limit, they flattered his ego and thus, unwittingly, laid a snare for his feet. Had he chosen the latter instead, he would have then been surrounded by men who challenged him, causing him to think through the potential consequences of his actions, men who would tolerate no compromise of character.

To maintain a life of moral purity, someone complementary to you is essential. You don't need a clone but a loving critic, someone whose advice you are willing to heed, someone you respect, someone who will be your greatest ally—and your greatest adversary if you adopt destructive moral practices. Ask God to help you find just such a person, and be sure to listen with you heart.

No Need to Be a Statistic

The world is full of dismal statistics regarding crumbling marriages and moral failure, but you need not be one of them. Determine now that you will honor the family, God's first institution, with a life of moral purity and marital fidelity. Purpose to live a holy and godly life. And guard your heart, filling it with the Word of God, fleeing enticements to sin against God and your family, fixing your vision on His plan for your life, and finding a genuine accountability partner.

Thinking It Through, Living It Out

1. To what extent have the issues of moral purity or marital fidelity been major issues in your life? Are you aware that immoral practices prior to marriage constitute sin against your future mate? In what areas of your moral life do you find the most struggles? Where do you fall most often? What do you think are the steps you can take to gain victory in those areas?

2. How would you rate your understanding and appreciation of the family? High? Average? Poor? How much has your own family background affected your thinking? If married, have you discussed with your spouse which view of the family is most appropriate and scriptural? If planning to marry, have you discussed God's view of the family with your future mate? How does your view of marriage and family affect your moral choices?

3. Since "the ways of man are before the eyes of the LORD" (Prov. 5:21), do you believe God is pleased with your moral choices each day? Displeased? Have you simply adopted some practices or habits that you know hinder your relationship with Him? How are these practices affecting your family? What are some positive steps you take each day as indications of your desire to live a holy life? Do your friends

and family consider you to be a person who aspires to holiness? Are they correct in their assessment?

4. What role does the prayerful reading of God's Word have in your daily life? Were you absolutely honest in answering that question? Do you find yourself growing through your study of God's Word? How long has it been since, by reading the Bible, you have become convicted of a specific sin, confessed, repented, and gained victory over it? Do you find that, more and more, specific Scriptures come to mind when you are being tempted to sin? Do they assist you in overcoming the temptation?

5. How clearly do you feel you understand God's plan for your life? Your family? Are you cooperating with Him in its achievement? Do you have someone in your life who genuinely holds you accountable? Who? When did you last visit with that person? Does this person know of your need for accountability? Is this person a godly and sincere individual? Have you shared with this person your desire to live a life of moral purity, marital fidelity, and Christlike love for your other family members?

The church is the bride of Christ, comprised of all the redeemed who will, one day, be taken to heaven by Him. By exalting Christ, resting on the sufficiency of His Word, and giving place to the ministry of the Spirit, the local church becomes the means by which spiritual growth is promoted and the ministry of Christ is brought to my family, my community, and the world.

I will support and will encourage my family to support our local church with faithful attendance, diligent service, generous and God-honoring giving, and loving cooperation (Matt. 16:18; Eph. 5:25; 4:11–16; Heb. 10:25).

CHAPTER FIVE

SERVING MY CHURCH

Ask people to describe "church," and you will get a variety of answers. For some, church is more of a place than a fellowship. For others, the association between church and a place is never made because, for differing reasons, they must meet in a wide variety of locations. Still others will tell you that their church is their life and all their activities revolve around the events on the schedule for each week. Then there are those for whom church is reserved for special days and occasions, a theological icing on a celebratory cake.

Members of God's Kingdom Family speak of the church as the bride of Christ, comprised of all the redeemed who will one day be caught up to heaven to spend eternity with Him. In the meantime they realize that their church is the local representation of the body of Christ. Members of their church are each uniquely gifted by the Spirit of God so that, in fellowship together, their community can experience Christ at work among them. They realize that their church is worthy of their faithful attendance, diligent service, generous and God-honoring giving, and loving cooperation.

Over the years the church has suffered many things at the hands of many misguided people. Members of God's Kingdom Family realize, however, that their church is comprised of people who, like them, will only be perfect someday in heaven. In the meantime, though often confronted with what's wrong with their church, they are more focused upon what's right with it. Look at the list and I think you will be impressed as well.

THE INTEGRITY OF OUR MASTER

Every age has suffered its ecclesiastical embarrassments. So much so, in fact, that some have chosen simply to write off the church as an absurd idea. "After all," they say, "look at all the hypocrites in the church!" Without attempting to fight that criticism with sarcasm (You've got to be smaller than the one behind whom you hide!), it is important to remember that the church is built upon Christ in whom there has never been, nor ever will be, the slightest compromise of integrity.

Take a trip with me back in time to the days immediately following Christ's ascension. Jerusalem is buzzing with news of the incredible events of Pentecost. The church in Jerusalem is expanding exponentially. The staid Jewish community along with its leadership has been turned upside down and is in a defensive mode. Now word has reached them of a miracle in which a man, lame from birth, has been healed. A crowd has gathered and Peter is preaching again, this time emphasizing Christ's resurrection. The Sadducees, longtime foes of the resurrection, wade into the fray and have them arrested.

After a night in jail, Peter and John now find themselves standing before the council. Filled with the Spirit, Peter speaks eloquently about what's right with the church. Listen in as he addresses the integrity of the Lord whom they serve: "Be it known unto you all, and to all the people of Israel, that by the name of Jesus Christ of Nazareth, whom ye crucified, whom God raised from the dead, even by him does this man stand here before you whole" (Acts 4:10 KJV).

Notice the "impressive credentials" of Peter's (and the church's) Master. He is:

"_Jesus_," the Deliverer

"_Christ_," the Anointed of God

"_Of Nazareth_," therefore, the "prophesied One"

"_Crucified_," having died for our sin

"_Raised_," having conquered death and been raised to eternal life

"_This man stands before you whole_," He is the Great Physician!

But in addition to these impressive credentials, Peter offers this important commentary: "This is the stone which was rejected by you builders, which has become the chief cornerstone" (Acts 4:11).

Peter's audience understood this terminology in both the practical and the theological sense. They knew, for instance, that the "chief cornerstone" was the first stone laid in a construction project. It would become the point of reference for all that followed. They also knew that it was designed to join together two important, load-bearing walls. All in all, they should have understood from the Scripture exactly what Peter was saying. "Jesus came first. He is the point of reference. He is the One who joins together and makes sense of the two great walls: the wall of the Old Testament, built upon the foundation of the prophets and the wall of the New Testament, built upon the foundation of the apostles" (see Eph. 2:20).

Recently I watched as, under intense verbal fire, an adherent of a non-Christian religion was forced to admit that its leader and founder of the faith had "made some mistakes." That can never be honestly said of Christ, our Chief Cornerstone. Throughout eternity His integrity, though under constant fire, has never been faulted. This is the Lord of the church comprised of members of His body, His Kingdom Family.

THE IMPORTANCE OF OUR MESSAGE

The singular message of each local church is the most important message any person will ever hear: "Nor is there salvation in any other, for there is no other name under heaven given among men by which we must be saved" (Acts 4:12).

This is an exciting Word that the world is desperate to hear. Occasionally I hear someone lament just how difficult it is to share the faith. In reality, this is a message that is bigger than any difficulty we might encounter in order to share it. People scarcely think of the difficulties encountered when warning others to flee a burning building or seek shelter in a storm. The significance of the message is reason enough to share it. Besides, more often than we imagine, people are eager to hear how they may have eternal life.

For years I have made a habit when dining in a restaurant to ask this simple question of the waiter or waitress: "When I pray, thanking God for this food, how may I pray for you?" Only rarely have I been refused an answer. Sometimes the individual returns to express gratitude and clarify the request. On other occasions they have literally pulled up a chair and opened up their hearts. And in more instances than I can recall, this simple question has opened the door for a witness that subsequently led to a decision to trust Christ! People want to hear this exciting, good news!

Some years ago I stopped by a cancer-ridden church member's home to assure him of my prayers. From his bed he said, "Pastor, have I ever shared my testimony with you?" I answered that I had heard it many times but would love to hear it again. After sharing his testimony he said, "Now, pastor, why don't you share yours with me?" I eagerly took the opportunity, knowing that I had also shared my conversion experience with him on many previous occasions. In closing, I said, "I'm so glad someone shared with me how I could have eternal life." Imagine my surprise when, out of a darkened corner, a hospice nurse whom I'd never noticed said, "I'd like that." And in a matter of minutes God's Kingdom Family welcomed a new addition!

But our message is more than an exciting word. It speaks of an exclusive way. "Nor is there salvation in any other, for there is no other name under heaven given among men by which we must be saved" (Acts 4:12). This adds supreme significance to our message. Christ is not simply *a* way to heaven, or even the *best* way, He is the *only* way (see John 14:6)! This means that as you, through your church, share the message of Christ, you are speaking of an issue that eclipses any discussion in a science laboratory, a hall of government, or a battlefield. While those deal with temporal issues, you are speaking of an issue of eternal significance. And this is the message of the church, God's Kingdom Family! It is in cooperation with members of your local church that this message is shared most effectively where you live and around the world.

THE IMPACT OF OUR MINISTRY

The message of the gospel is a message of life-transforming power. When you, and other members of your church, begin sharing this message, it makes a phenomenal impact, explainable only in terms of God! This is the ministry of your church, a ministry that leaves the world with nothing of similar comparison, a ministry that often overwhelms any criticism and shuts the mouth of the skeptic.

Ours is a ministry that makes *somebodies* out of *nobodies*. That's what the Sanhedrin concluded as they sized up Peter and John. "Now when they saw the boldness of Peter and John, and perceived that they were unlearned and ignorant men, they marvelled; and they took knowledge of them, that they had been with Jesus" (Acts 4:13 KJV).

Peter and John were, to put it mildly, out of place in Jerusalem. As rough fishermen from up north, they were unaccustomed to city ways not to mention a trial by the religious big shots of their day. Yet they had seized control of the trial, and now it was their accusers who were in a panic. Where did this boldness come from? In the words of the Sanhedrin, "They had been with Jesus." That's the impact of our ministry!

Once, while visiting on a college campus where I served as trustee, I was approached by a winsome, bright-eyed African-American coed. "Brother Tom, do you remember me?" she asked. Looking into her face, a flood of memories almost overwhelmed me. Yes, I did remember her. I remembered when our bus ministers found her in an abusive home with alcoholic parents. I remembered when she asked for an onion off of a Thanksgiving display because "me and my brother have had nuthin' to eat." I remembered her mischievousness at church and later at camp. I remembered when she had trusted Christ and then followed Him in baptism. Oh yes, I remembered her!

But I was unprepared for what came next. "Brother Tom," she said, "do you know I am about to graduate from this school right up at the top of my class!" Here was someone destined to become a *nobody*, who through Christ, had become a *somebody*. I tell this story to people who sometimes question whether they should support their church with their time, money, prayers, and service. It is a perfect illustration of the impact of our ministry!

The church also shares a ministry that enables *broken lives* to become *beautiful lives*. This was what really perplexed the council. "And seeing the man who had been healed standing with them, they could say nothing against it" (Acts 4:14).

As a friend of mine says, "The person with the argument is always at the mercy of the person with the experience." Here was a man with an experience. Through the ministry of these two ordinary men from the church in Jerusalem, a broken life had become a beautiful life. That's the impact of our ministry!

One of the great privileges of every pastor is looking out across the congregation and knowing how God has taken broken lives and made them beautiful. In a recent service I looked down to see a beautiful family seated on the front row of our church. They had come to dedicate themselves to the Lord, seeking His grace in rearing their most recent addition to the Lord. As I looked at them, they were so winsome and radiant that I literally forgot the years when both husband and wife had broken and shattered lives. She had been a practicing lesbian and the daughter of a practicing lesbian. He had come to know Christ and then enrolled in a soul-winning training course. They met while he was out on soul-winning visitation, and he had led her to Christ. They had sub-sequently married and become faithful in church. Now, having both been delivered by the power of Christ, they had come to the altar once again to dedicate themselves and their child to the Lord. Lives, once broken, had become beautiful. This is the impact of our ministry!

THE INSPIRATION FOR OUR MISSION

As a member of a local church, Kingdom Family members are inspired to participate in a unique combination of ministry and missions. It is more than a matter of obeying Christ's command to "make disciples of all nations." They operate from an inner com-pulsion that springs out of their own personal experience with Christ. They cannot help but share the good news because it has meant so much to them.

This was what the council discovered as they questioned and then threatened Peter and John. Their inspiration did not spring from selfish purposes. It was from on high, the work of God's Spirit in their lives!

But when they had commanded them to go aside out
of the council, they conferred among themselves, saying,
"What shall we do to these men? For, indeed, that a
notable miracle has been done through them is evident to

all who dwell in Jerusalem, and we cannot deny it. But so
that it spreads no further among the people, let us
severely threaten them, that from now on they speak to
no man in this name." And they called them and commanded them not to speak at all nor teach in the name of
Jesus. But Peter and John answered and said to them,
"Whether it is right in the sight of God to listen to you
more than God, you judge. For we cannot but speak the
things which we have seen and heard." (Acts 4:15–20)

There you see how their actions were inspired by both the
command of the Lord ("the things we have seen and heard")
and the inner compulsion of God's Spirit ("we cannot help but
speak").

For many years I have sent out prayer letters each day to a
number of church members. I tell them that on a specific date in
the future I will be praying for them by name, and I ask them to
provide me with a list of their prayer concerns. Reading those letters each day has become an incredible blessing to me. It has
helped me get to know my flock in ways far deeper than I could
ever know them through casual conversation.

I once received a letter from a young lady in our singles ministry, asking prayer as she began a new route in our bus ministry.
In the letter she shared that she was a product of our church's outreach to students. She spoke of a home situation that included an
absent father and an unsaved mother whose boyfriends abused
her. She recalled how, prior to meeting Christ, she often had
thoughts of suicide. But all that changed when she came to know
Jesus as Lord and Savior. Now she had a burden for children who
like herself needed the transforming touch of Christ. No one was
twisting her arm to get her involved in reaching out to others
through her church. She had been praying for the opportunity.
Compelled by the love of Christ, she would be serving Him! In
other words, like Peter and John, she "couldn't help but speak and
teach the things she had seen of Christ." That's the inspiration for
our mission.

THE IMMINENCE OF OUR MASTER'S RETURN

Members of God's Kingdom Family live with the knowledge and deep conviction that Christ's return is imminent or on the horizon. They eagerly anticipate that moment when He calls the church, His bride, unto Himself. And they know that, in the meantime, they are to heed the example of Christ, who said, "I must work the works of Him Who sent me while it is day; the night is coming when no one can work" (John 9:4). Like Christ, we are on a mission, *His* mission, and our time is limited.

Peter and John could recall that incredible moment that had taken place only a few days earlier. It was an event that set the stage for their ministry and defined the urgency of the hour. Christ had spoken to them, assuring them that the Holy Spirit would come and enable them to fulfill His commission.

> And when he had spoken these things, while they
> beheld, he was taken up; and a cloud received him
> out of their sight. And while they looked stedfastly
> toward heaven as he went up, behold, two men stood
> by them in white apparel; which also said, Ye men of
> Galilee, why stand ye gazing up into heaven? this same
> Jesus, which is taken up from you into heaven, shall so
> come in like manner as ye have seen him go into heaven.
> (Acts 1:9–11 KJV)

The imminence of Christ's return is worthy of both our *reflection* and our *resolve*. We should often reflect upon the fact that Christ never breaks a promise. Just as He has fulfilled all others, He will fulfill this as well. He is coming. His coming will be with startling and surprising immediacy. It should not catch us sleeping, inattentive to the work assigned us. Our resolve should be as His, a resolve echoed in the hymn "Work for the Night Is Coming."

While living in Africa, we were privileged to have working on our grounds a young man named Petros Nkala. He was bright, energetic, and thrilled to have both work to do and a place to live. Prior to working for us he had spent most nights homeless, sleeping in a ditch. Petros came to saving faith in Christ while working and living with us. Over a period of time we increasingly trusted him with responsibilities that he fulfilled in a timely manner.

Once, while we were preparing for an extended trip to South Africa, I took Petros on a walk around the grounds, pointing out specific work to be done each day. I told him that the responsibility would not be overwhelming *if* he did his work each day. Then I told him exactly when we would return and what needed to be done in order to prepare for our arrival.

For some reason that I have since forgotten, we returned home several days early, only to find the work incomplete and Petros missing. At first I worried that some mishap might have occurred. But then I decided not to panic, at least until the day we had originally scheduled for our return. Perhaps Petros had simply not done the work each day, assuming it could all be completed in a few hours before our arrival. Soon my suspicions were confirmed. Imagine Petros's surprise when, with a whistle he parked his bicycle by our gate, reached to open it, and saw me standing by my car! (You can use your imagination and take it from here!)

Petros was no different, however, from any professing believer who is simply not stirred into action by the imminence of Christ's return. One day—and I believe that day will be soon—Christ will come to call His bride unto Himself. Like Peter and John, and all members of God's Kingdom Family, we cannot help but be stirred by thoughts of His soon return!

WORTH YOUR FAITHFUL SUPPORT

While reflecting on the things that are right about the church,
- The integrity of our Master
- The importance of our message
- The impact of our ministry
- The inspiration for our mission
- The imminence of our Master's return

you cannot help but rejoice in the privilege of being part of your local church, the body of Christ right where you live. It is indeed worthy of your faithful attendance, diligent service, generous and God-honoring giving, and loving cooperation. Does that mean your church is perfect in every way? Of course not! That will not happen until our Lord calls His church home to heaven. But Christ gave Himself for His church, and we should do no less!

Someone once told of an imaginary interview between a popular newscaster and Noah, conducted shortly after the floodwaters had subsided. The newscaster was asking Noah about living condtions on the ark. "Wasn't it smelly? Dark? Humid? Crowded? Dirty?" he asked. "Sure," replied Noah, "but it was the best ship floating!"

The church is the best ship floating and the only ship that Christ will bring home to Himself. God's Kingdom Family looks forward to that day! And in the meantime we will be found faithful to it!

Thinking It Through, Living It Out

1. Are you a member of a local church? How would you describe your involvement in your local church? Do you attend faithfully? Serve diligently? Give generously? Cooperate lovingly? Are you gladly accountable to others in your fellowship for the manner in which you live out your faith?

2. Do you have a network of positive-thinking friends who also love the church and support it? Do they speak well of their church? Do they hold positions of ministry and service? Would you consider them as friends who build you up in your faith? Have you grown in your faith in recent years?

3. How actively are you involved in the support of world missions through your church? Local outreach? Have you ever taken training to increase your own effectiveness in sharing your faith? Like Peter and John, do you feel inwardly compelled and excited about sharing Christ with others?

4. Are you spiritually growing with others in your church? Do you know their testimonies? Do they know yours? How often do you actually pray together with others in your church? When opportunities arise, are you happy to give spontaneously and sacrificially for the support of missions and outreach?

5. How has your involvement and support of your church changed in the last several years? Are you more supportive and involved? Less supportive? Do you find it easier to let others carry the load? Do you find yourself looking for opportunities to serve? Do you reflect often on the fact that Christ is coming soon? Does that thought change the way you behave?

Time is a resource given to each person by God. My use of it, especially in matters related to my family, reflects my esteem for God. One day I will give an account to Him for how I have spent the time He entrusted to me. As I order my life in concert with His will, I will have sufficient time for personal growth through prayer, for the study of God's Word, and for fulfilling every God-given responsibility related to my family (Eph. 5:15; 2 Tim. 3:16–17; Deut. 6:6–7; Luke 18:16; Ps. 90:12).

CHAPTER SIX

USING TIME WISELY

Time management, ordering your priorities, making the most of your time, how to make your minutes count, distinguishing the important from the urgent—the popularity of subjects like these indicates the struggle we each experience when seeking to use our time wisely. The saying, "I've got places to go, people to see, and things to do!" is descriptive of many in a society that literally bombards us with claims on our time. How often have you invited someone to church only to hear, "I'm sorry, man. That's the only day I have a little time for myself! A man's gotta have a little break every now and then, you know."

Ironically, although the best instructions anywhere on the wise use of time are available in God's timeless book, the Bible, many dedicated Christians confess to being as pushed and weary as anyone else. They even admit that they just don't have time for a consistent, daily time in the Word of God and for prayer. The popularity of fast-food service has created a similar demand for "church on the go." The simple fact is that, for most people, their world is the primary determinant when it comes to the way they spend their time.

"Stop the world, I want to get off!" Those often repeated words describe the longing lurking in the hearts of many. In the meantime, many sign up for still another time management seminar, spending a few more days and dollars in an attempt to find the secrets that will set them free from the time trap. The good news is that such secrets exist and are available to anyone willing to hear. They are found in God's timeless book, the Bible.

A Limited, Nonrenewable Resource

Time, like everything else God has created, is a limited, non-renewable resource that has been entrusted to us by God. As such, it demands as much attention to stewardship as everything else entrusted to us (money, opportunities, abilities, etc.). Many people fail to see it as such, yet a little reflection will reveal the truth of that statement.

Yes, time is a created resource meant for our benefit and God's glory. We actually measure time by the things God has placed in His created order. The rotating of the earth on its axis, the revolution of the earth around the sun, the atomic tick of a quartz crystal are just a few of the means by which we measure time. Each one is a function of God's creative act. God, the Creator, of course, is outside or beyond that which He has created. Time is normal to us in this world where everything has a beginning and an end. But it is abnormal to God, who has no such created boundaries and lives eternally.

Think for a moment about the nonrenewable aspect of time. That characteristic is actually even more true of time than it is of some other resources such as money. "It takes money to make money!" That statement illustrates that money is actually a renewable resource. Once spent, there are actually methods, such as hard work, by which money can be replaced. Our time, on the other hand, may be extended by careful use—healthy diet, rest, etc.—but once spent it cannot be replaced.

Because time is a resource entrusted to our care, it is imperative to know just what is involved in the proper stewardship or wise use of it. After all, each of us will one day render an account to God for the manner in which we have spent our time. Will we have used it wisely? Will God have been honored by the manner in which we spent our time? The key is to find how to get the most benefit and give God the most glory with the time we have.

Some people have a remarkable capacity for living life to the fullest and leaving a legacy that actually lasts far beyond their years. Others seem to quit living before their lives come to an end. And, unfortunately, the impact of their lives is scarcely felt beyond their funeral, if even for that long.

I have a friend who is fond of reminding his aging counterparts that "life is not over until it's over!" That's his way of reminding them—and himself, in the process—that God has a purpose for us until we draw our last breath. And He will hold us accountable for the way we use every minute entrusted to us. On the days when I am tempted to forget that principle, I recall that one grandfather (on my father's side) preached his last sermon just two days before his death at age ninety-two. My other grandfather (on my mother's side) farmed until the age of ninety-five. That year he actually considered planting seedlings for a future timber harvest!

Taking the experience of my two grandfathers into account, I must realize that it's possible I may have as many years of active ministry ahead of me as behind. And I've been a minister for forty years! On the other hand, God may have an entirely different plan. He may know that I should be thinking about years or months of service rather than decades. The issue is not how long I may have to live but how I live out the balance of my life. Will I bring glory to God by the wise use of my time? And will you? The psalmist addresses this issue with the prayer that God will "teach us to number [or count as valuable] our days, that we may apply our hearts unto wisdom" (Ps. 90:12 KJV).

TIME MUST BE REDEEMED

Remember the statement, "An idle mind is the devil's playground"? Time, like everything else in God's created order, fell under the curse of sin when Adam and Eve rebelled against God in the garden of Eden. And, like everything else, it must be "redeemed" if it is to bring glory to God and benefit to man. In other words, time has a natural tendency to run toward evil and must be claimed back by the believer on the basis of Christ's atoning work on the cross. You must take deliberate steps to use time wisely. Your adversary already has plans for your time, and you must actively redeem or rescue it from him. That is why the apostle Paul exhorts us to walk wisely, "redeeming the time, because the days are evil" (Eph. 5:16 KJV).

Once, after spending a long period of meditation on the above passage, I had a dream during the night that followed. (Don't worry! I'll use that dream to illustrate my theology, not establish it. After all, it might have been that extra helping of chili!) In my dream I was standing on the side of a mountain, looking down upon a great valley below. In that valley I saw a huge multitude of unusual animals of many shapes and sizes. A closer inspection revealed that the animals were actually representations of time. There were huge, elephant-sized years, smaller cattle that represented months, even smaller creatures representing weeks and days. Flying creatures like birds and insects represented minutes and seconds! (I know this sounds strange, but please stay with me!)

As I watched the vast assemblage below me, I noticed that they all seemed to be moving in the same direction. In fact, as I looked toward the far end of the valley, I saw someone standing by an open gate. I became agitated because whoever was by that gate was allowing my time to get out without my permission! I hurried down to stop him.

"Who are you?" I asked.

"Why," he said, "I'm the devil!"

"What are you doing with all my time?" I urged.

"I'm a time rustler, and I've got good use for all this time," he said laconically. I could almost see a weed between his teeth.

"Well, you can't have it!" I protested.

"Why not?" he asked. "After all, you don't have any plans for it!"

I awakened from my dream, disturbed by the reality that the adversary does already have plans for the time entrusted me. In fact, he has a multibillion-dollar operation already in place for the purpose of laying claim to my time. Sadly, the natural tendency of my time is to move toward the gate that Satan has opened. The only solution is for me to redeem the time (literally, to go to the market and buy it off the slave stand) because "the days are evil" (by their very nature). But how can I do this?

TIME MUST BE ORDERED ACCORDING TO GOD'S WILL

In our efforts to redeem the time, God wants us to be "not unwise, but understanding what the will of the Lord is" (Eph. 5:17 KJV). This is the only possible way for us to conduct ourselves properly, "not as fools, but as wise" men instead (Eph. 5:15). Proverbs 3:5–6 tells us how we can have God-directed paths: "Trust in the LORD with all your heart, and lean not on your own understanding; In all your ways acknowledge Him, _and he shall direct your paths_" (emphasis mine).

Radical devotion—As members of God's Kingdom Family, we should use our time in a manner that reflects our radical devotion to the Lord. We are to trust in the Lord with all our heart. The choice of our priorities will be guided by our faith in Christ and our deep love for Him. William Borden, one of Yale's most enterprising students of the last century, turned his back on a lucrative career in business, headed to Egypt to join a team of missionaries, and was suddenly stricken with a disease that would quickly claim his life. Friends, who doubted his call in the first place, wrote letters urging him to return home. His reply was simple, his response reading, "No regret, no remorse, no return." Was he a poor steward of his brief life? Literally thousands of people have been stirred to mission service by his example of sacrifice and devotion.

Just as our love for the Lord affects the manner in which we spend our money, it also effects the way we spend our time. On many occasions I have had the privilege of serving with others on short-term overseas mission projects. In virtually every instance there are people on the team who are using their scarce annual vacation leave afforded by their employer. Instead of lavishing those days upon themselves and their needs, they have chosen to use the time in a manner that is both spiritually significant and eternally rewarding. Using personal time for evangelism training, teaching Bible classes, working in special ministries, church visitation, reaching out to your neighbors—these and other uses indicate a radical, selfless devotion to the Lord.

Reasoned departure—The wise use of our time will also require a reasoned departure from our own assumptions so that we may operate from the basis of God's point of view. We will "lean not unto (our) own understanding." We will reject any counsel that encourages us to violate the clear principles of God as revealed in the Scripture, choosing instead to utilize our time in a fashion that pleases our Lord.

The award-winning film *Chariots of Fire* focused on the matter of Eric Liddell's devotion to the Lord and the manner in which that devotion led him to depart from a much heralded competition in the 1924 Olympics. Liddell chose to withdraw from a Sunday running of the one hundred meter, a race he was almost certain to win, in order to honor the Lord on His day. That kind of dedication to principle, and the manner in which it guided his use of time, later sustained him on the mission field and then as a prisoner of war. God honored Liddell's departure from the worldly norm far beyond all expectation, and he returned to England, a hero, having won the bronze medal in the two hundred meter and the gold in the four hundred meter.

The prophet Daniel had a significant influence on at least two worldly regimes in his day—first, the Babylonian, then the Medo-Persian Empire. In both instances, though a leader whose counsel was highly regarded, his personal use of time was significantly different from the norms of the society in which he lived. In fact, Daniel is the only individual other than Christ (see John 18:2) whose life was plotted against on the basis of his use of time for prayer. The moment a decree was signed forbidding prayer to anyone other than Darius, Daniel went to his home and prayed three times a day as he always did before (see Dan. 6:10). As in the case of his physical diet under Babylonian rule, Daniel was unafraid and unashamed to depart from the cultural norm in order to obey God. Yet he conducted himself with such reason, grace, and trustworthiness that his counsel was often sought and heeded.

Resolute discipline—Using our time wisely also demands a resolute discipline. Our conduct will be guided by the lordship of Christ over our lives and our constant desire to enter into fellowship with Him. We will seek to acknowledge Him (literally, to know by observing Him) in all our ways. Our use of time will be principled on the one hand yet dynamically guided by our constant, disciplined looking to Him on the other. When reading the Psalms, for instance, we see this practice in action. David repeatedly speaks of "seeking God's face," seeking Him "early," communing with Him "in the night watches," worshiping Him both "evening and morning."

It would be difficult to find someone God has used in a significant fashion who was not also consistent in the matter of daily acknowledging the Lord, bringing Him into the issues of life, seeking His direction, and acting in concert with it. Martin Luther spoke of having so much to do that he could not think of beginning without spending at least four hours in prayer. Hudson Taylor, mission pioneer and founder of the China Inland Mission (now called the Overseas Missionary Fellowship), spent grueling days in travel;

yet those with him wrote of seeing the flicker of a candle behind his curtain around two o'clock each morning and knowing he was having his time with God. David Brainerd's diary tells of nights of prayer in spite of a debilitating illness that took his life at the age of thirty. No wonder it is said that God brought revival among the Native Americans along the eastern seaboard on the wings of Brainerd's prayers. John Hyde of India writes of winning to Christ first one, then two, and ultimately an average of four persons each day, after his mornings spent in prayer.

God has promised that we can have His direction for our paths! In other words, we can redeem the time, using it for our benefit and His glory. It is a matter of acknowledging Him "in all our ways," whether the seemingly insignificant or the obviously important. Sometimes we have the tendency to think that the things done to God's glory must be big, significant, attention grabbing, and life impacting. In reality, God is not so much honored by our doing *some* great things as He is in our doing *all* the things He puts before us in a great way. Thus the importance of practicing the discipline of acknowledging Him, moment by moment.

SUFFICIENT TIME

How often have you heard someone lament, "I just don't have enough hours in the day!" or, "There is no way I can do all that I must do in the time available." Members of God's Kingdom Family have made an exciting discovery when following God's principles for the wise use of time. As we order our lives in concert with God's will, we have sufficient time for personal growth through prayer, for the study of God's Word, and for fulfilling every God-given responsibility related to our family. That is an awesome prospect!

I have a pastor friend who has an incredible knack for accomplishing a multitude of things without ever seeming pushed, hurried, or distressed. Over the years I have carefully observed his life. Like Jesus, he has a remarkable capacity for walking slowly and attentively among His flock. And, like Jesus, it seems that at the end of each day, he has properly dealt with all the issues "heaped on his plate" throughout that day's course. He has time for his family, time for an appropriate amount of recreational activity, time to relate with others outside the normal traffic pattern of his life. According to him, there is always time for those things that are important if a man will take time for that which is most important—the practice of consistent, early devotion. During this time, he relates, God brings order and discipline to a life that would cause the average person to panic.

My friend says that he suffers occasional crashes when everything seems out of control. But these occur, according to him, when for some reason he has been less than attentive to the Lord in his early morning devotions. These periodic moments when life seems to fall down around his ears are viewed by him as God's call to worship, and he seeks to return quickly to the practice that has sustained him through the years.

When our children were young and in school, ranging from grade school through high school, Jeannie and I realized the need for a similar anchor that would keep our family from drifting into the world's way of abusing time. We each had a long practice of having our own morning time of devotion. But we realized a need for a daily time together, just the two of us, and time with our family. In our own world, there were (and are) many claims upon our evenings. There were, of course, church activities and social responsibilities. Having children in school and sports only complicated the issue. We could see that things would soon get out of hand. And the biggest danger lay in the possibility that we would omit the important things so that we might attend to those that were seemingly more urgent.

We decided that this was a problem worthy of serious, prayerful consideration. At an annual retreat that Jeannie and I have been privileged to enjoy together for many years, we made the issue of our daily time together, along with our need for a daily family time, the major issue of discussion. Through prayer and prolonged periods of discussion, we finally arrived at a plan that would suit our schedule and our children's.

First, we determined that after we had each engaged in our own personal time of devotion each morning, we would then meet together, just the two of us, for thirty minutes. This was a face-to-face meeting in which we discussed our family needs and schedule, a time for making specific decisions, a time to review the schedule for the day, and a time for giving each other our undivided attention. (For us, this time was from 6:00 to 6:30 A.M., Monday–Friday.) After this time together, while Jeannie prepared breakfast, the children and I would prepare for school and work. Then we ate breakfast together as a family at a set time. (For us this was 7:00 A.M.) The children knew this was the time for breakfast together, and everyone was expected to be present. At the table we read a brief passage of Scripture, prayed, and then discussed the events of the day. This was also a time for Jeannie and me to share decisions affecting our family, decisions we had made together.

When I have shared our own family's schedule, some people have commented that, in their situation, such a schedule would simply not be practical. (Perhaps someone must leave very early for work each day, for example.) The issue is not necessarily using the schedule we found helpful for our family. It is, through prayer and discussion, finding a time that will be a similar anchor for your family each day. This is helpful even if some members of your family have yet to meet Christ and receive Him as Savior. A daily time, personally and for your family, is an incredible and practical tool for using time wisely.

Several years ago our church's tape ministry received a request from a lady who lived in a remote town in a western state. She had heard our radio broadcast and wondered if we would send tapes that she could play while she and her family were having breakfast together each morning. "My husband and children are not believers," she wrote, "so anything you could send me would be of great help." The request was processed, and we began sending her the tapes she requested.

Some time later I drove into the church parking lot early one Sunday morning just behind another car with an out-of-state license. As the husband and wife got out of the car, I introduced myself to them and asked where they were from. When they told me, I commented that interestingly we had been sending some tapes to a lady in the same area. Then, in my typical foot-in-mouth fashion, I said, "She's got a husband who is as lost as a goose in a snowstorm!"

"Yep. I know," replied the man, "I'm him, and that's her!" (I gulped and did my practiced shuck-and-jive routine.) "Aw, don't worry, preacher," he continued, "I was out on a cattle-buying trip and began thinking about those tapes we've been listening to every morning. I called my wife, and asked her to catch a plane and meet me here. Now can you tell me how to get saved?"

God has incredible blessings in store for those who are committed to using their time wisely! You will one day give an account to Him for how you have spent this nonrenewable resource entrusted to your care. By the manner in which you use it you can bring glory and honor to your Lord. In the meantime, just like the couple above, through the wise use of it, you will have time for your own personal growth and for fulfilling every responsibility God has assigned you, including Kingdom Family!

Thinking It Through, Living It Out

1. How often do you think through the manner in which you are spending the nonrenewable resource called "time"? Do you take time to consider prayerfully how God would have you oversee the time entrusted you? Are you aware that, one day, you will give an account to Him for the stewardship of your time? Since you cannot relive your past, are there definite steps you should take to make the most of your future?

2. Do you regularly set aside time for planning out the way you will spend your time? If others are to be involved (your spouse, family, etc.), do you involve them in this planning?

How aware are you of the events in the lives of those who mean most to you? Do you leave the plans for your family up to someone else? If married, do you have a specific time each day when you and your spouse discuss matters affecting your family, pray for wisdom, and make decisions together?

3. What specific steps are you taking to "redeem the time," to claim it for God's glory and your benefit? Are specific activities eating up your time yet producing little that is of wholesome value? Are there activities you need to omit? Do you have trouble saying no to others' requests simply because you have not planned out your time to include things of utmost importance? Do you find yourself giving more time to things that seem urgent and less time to those things you know are genuinely important?

4. Are you aware that you have sufficient time to fulfill all the responsibilities God has assigned you, including responsibilities for personal devotion, work, church, and family? Do you find yourself complaining that you have too much to do? Too much on your plate? Too few hours in the day? Would other people describe you as calm? Focused? Effective? Or would they describe you as frustrated? Distracted? Ineffective?

5. Do you set aside time each day for personal devotion? What time do you find best for your personal devotion time? Are you consistent in meeting with the Lord at this time? Have you given serious thought to ways of making this devotion time more effective? If you live with other family members, do you meet with them each day? Is there a devotional anchor in your family? Do your decisions as a family reflect that they are born out of serious prayer and discussion? How can you make your family devotion time more effective?

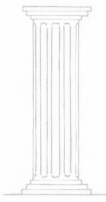
God has provided material resources so that I may glorify Him through the exercise of faithful stewardship over them. I will be held accountable for this stewardship. Therefore, I will diligently seek my Master's best interests in the way I earn money, expend it for life's needs, use it to touch the lives of others, and give it for the support of His work through my local church (Luke 6:38; 12:48; Gen. 1:28; Prov. 3:9–10; 2 Cor. 9:7; 1 Cor. 4:22; 16:1–2; Mal. 3:8–11).

CHAPTER SEVEN

PRACTICING BIBLICAL STEWARDSHIP

Few issues arouse such interest as those that touch on the management of our personal finances. Many families are awash in a sea of red ink, paddling furiously but drowning in personal indebtedness. Consumer (or credit card) debt is at an all-time high, as are applications for bankruptcy. That practice, which once was considered to be avoided at all costs, has now become the accepted manner of deliverance from indebtedness that has resulted from poor decisions and even poorer discipline.

The ultimate irony is the manner in which society actually encourages indebtedness. It is not unusual for an individual to spend hours each month in the creative juggling of indebtedness from one account to another. But in the mailbox, along with threatening notices for long-overdue bills, the same individual finds a daily assortment of invitations to enroll in new credit accounts for which he is already preapproved. Companies are running out of metals with which to solicit new account holders. There's undoubtedly a titanium card in your future, since silver, gold, and platinum have run their course.

Members of God's Kingdom Family take a more serious and Bible-centered approach to the management of the resources entrusted to them. They seek their Master's best interest in the way they earn, spend, and use their resources. They realize that good stewardship is the result of a commitment to specific biblical principles, which they diligently seek to employ. While many in God's Kingdom Family begin their stewardship pilgrimage in serious difficulty, they have discovered that following God's principles provides a way out as well as a way up. By adherence to these principles, they are now touching the lives of many others for the kingdom's sake and giving faithful, generous support to their local church. They have discovered that good stewardship is, in fact, a practice that makes life an exhilarating adventure in the cause of Christ, an adventure of earthly impact and eternal significance.

On the following pages you will be examining specific principles which, if followed, will enable you to exercise wise and biblical stewardship over your resources. For your benefit I have placed these principles into three main groups: (1) The Principles of Reverence, (2) The Principles of Responsibility, and (3) The Principles of Restoration. Finally, you will see the rewards God offers to those who practice wise stewardship.

Those who are in a financial pinch at the moment may be tempted to turn immediately to the section on restoration. I urge you to resist that temptation and take the time to deal with each principle in sequence. As you read through each principle, stop, reflect, and let God speak to your heart, then agree with Him before moving to the next principle.

PRINCIPLES OF REVERENCE

Stewardship must be approached with a spirit of reverence and respect. It is, at its heart, a matter of relationship. In other words, the way we handle the resources entrusted to us speaks volumes about our respect for the One who has assigned them to our care.

A local automobile dealership goes to great pains to illustrate the value they place on their customers. Taking your vehicle to them for even the simplest repair, you will discover that they have placed a protective covering over the seats and on the floor. When you return for your vehicle, they bring it to you repaired, washed, and with the interior vacuumed. It is their way of saying, "The manner in which we care for your vehicle is our way of showing appreciation for you, our customer." Their customers get more than a repaired car; they get respect! No wonder they are repeatedly rewarded for their customer service!

Principle 1: God owns everything; we own nothing. I once attended a seminar in which Christian principles of stewardship were discussed. The speaker made a great deal over the practice of going through one's house or business, and, item by item, transferring ownership to God. While I appreciated the sentiment, there was in his suggestion a basic theological flaw. He seemed to suggest that until we followed this practice the ownership remained ours. Perhaps a better plan would simply be to acknowledge God's pre-existing ownership of each item rather than transfer its title to Him.

National forests don't belong to the nation. State parks don't belong to the state. County roads don't belong to the county. Your house, possessions, family, time, abilities, even your own body belong to God and should be treated as such.

The earth is the LORD's, . . . for He has founded it. (Ps. 24:1–2)

Behold, the heaven and the heaven of heavens is the LORD's. (Deut. 10:14 KJV)

"The silver . . . and the gold is Mine," says the LORD of hosts. (Hag. 2:8)

> By Him all things were created . . . and for Him.
> (Col. 1:16)
> The world is mine, and the fulness thereof.
> (Ps. 50:12 KJV)

As a young boy, I was taken under the wing of a next-door neighbor who felt that all boys my age should grow up with a love for baseball. We spent endless hours playing catch, looking over baseball cards, listening to games on the radio, and actually going to a few when time and money afforded. He ate, slept, and lived the game. One afternoon our ball finally gave up the ghost. We had taped up the torn stitches and scuffed rawhide, but its use had come to an end. I didn't have another ball, and neither did he. Well, almost. Asking me to stay in the front yard, he went inside, returning a few minutes later with a perfectly good baseball, now browned with age.

"I guess we can use this," my neighbor and friend said wistfully. "It's a home run ball hit by Mickey Mantle over the center-field fence. I caught it on the second bounce in the bleachers."

I was almost afraid to touch the ball, much less throw it. To me it was more valuable than silver or gold. The last thing I wanted to do was throw an errant pitch that would land the ball in the street or against the fence. And Micky Mantle's fingerprints weren't even on the ball! He had simply hit it!

God says, "My fingerprints are on everything that exists!" What is in your hands has not been entrusted to your care by a baseball star who struggled with alcoholism, only turning to Christ in his latter years. What you have in your hands was entrusted to you by the God of the universe, the One who made you along with everything else in all of creation, the One who has provided for your salvation, the One to whom you must give an ultimate account. Are you showing reverence for Him by the manner in which you oversee what He has entrusted to your care?

Principle 2: God has designated us as the overseers of that which belongs to Him. The word *steward* means "overseer." A steward does not own; he oversees what is owned by another.

Theft is claiming as yours what actually belongs to someone else. A steward does not have to steal in order to enjoy what belongs to his master. He must use what has been entrusted to him in a manner that honors his master, his master's desires, his master's ownership.

God has said that what He has created is for His glory and our benefit. We have the privilege of being stewards over His creation.

> God blessed them, and God said unto them, Be fruitful, and multiply, and replenish the earth, and subdue it: and have dominion over the fish of the sea, and over the fowl of the air, and over every living thing that moveth upon the earth. (Gen. 1:28 KJV)

> You have made him to have dominion over the works of Your hands; You have put all things under his feet. (Ps. 8:6)

Your stewardship is a position distinctly assigned to you by God. You have a choice only in regard to the manner in which you perform your responsibility. Like it or not, you are a steward. Have you ever taken time to thank God for the privilege of being a steward over that which belongs to Him?

Principle 3: When we act responsibly as overseers, God provides for every need. Nothing delights the heart of a master so much as a steward who acts responsibly. Faithfulness to the master's best interest is the single most important requirement of a steward. In fact, Scripture reminds us that "it is required in stewards that a man be found faithful" (1 Cor. 4:2). As with every stewardship, faithfulness has its rewards. God promises that those who are faithful in their stewardship over His creation will have every need met and every godly desire satisfied.

> But seek first the kingdom of God and His righteousness, and all these things shall be added to you. (Matt. 6:33)

> But my God shall supply all your need according to his riches in glory by Christ Jesus. (Phil. 4:19 KJV)

> I have been young, and now am old; yet I have not
> seen the righteous forsaken, Nor his descendants begging
> bread. (Ps. 37:25)

In the Shepherd Psalm (Ps. 23), David reminds us that our Good Shepherd "leads [us] in paths of righteousness for His name's sake." In other words, the Lord's reputation is staked in some fashion on the manner in which He cares for His sheep. A friend of mine once reminded me that I have as much as God can trust me with. That's a sobering thought! Are you confident that God is not only capable but also willing to meet every need of your life and fulfill every godly desire of your heart? Do you see how His answer for your need is directly related to the manner in which you exercise your stewardship?

Principle 4: We will each give an account for our stewardship. The basis on which your stewardship will be judged may be summed up in this question: How have you used what has been entrusted to your care? You will not be judged for that which has not been entrusted to you. This judgment will take into account all you have been given: material resources, physical bodies, opportunities, abilities, spiritual giftedness, and time.

> For we must all appear before the judgment seat of
> Christ, that each one may receive the things done in the
> body, according to what he has done, whether good or
> bad. (2 Cor. 5:10)

> For if there is first a willing mind, it is accepted
> according to what one has, and not according to what he
> does not have. (2 Cor. 8:12)

> Moreover it is required in stewards that one be found
> faithful. (1 Cor. 4:2)

> To whom much is given, from him much will be
> required. (Luke 12:48)

In His kingdom parables, Jesus makes frequent use of the stewardship analogy as a picture of our relationship to Him. Reading them, we cannot miss the fact that, as believers, we must ultimately give an account for the manner in which we have used what He has entrusted to our care. It would be wise to take an inventory of all God has entrusted to you in every area of your life. How faithfully are you discharging your stewardship over these gifts?

PRINCIPLES OF RESPONSIBILITY

Since members of God's Kingdom Family must ultimately give an account for what they have done with what they have been given, it is important to know what our Master expects of us. Our Lord does not leave us guessing when it comes to His standards. They are clearly spelled out for us in the Scripture. These are the Principles of Responsibility, and they describe the manner in which we are to perform our stewardship.

Principle 1: As stewards, our primary responsibility is to glorify God. Glorifying the Lord means, literally, to make Him look good. We do this by overseeing what He has entrusted to our care with His best interest in mind. I once purchased a coat only to discover the following note tucked away in its pocket. "This article of clothing," read the note, "was subjected to a rigorous inspection process which included many different tests of its quality both in material and construction. It was only after successfully meeting our standards that we were willing to attach our label to the inside." This was their way of saying, "Our name stands for high quality." Our Lord's name stands for something as well, and we should perform our responsibilities in a manner suited to the King of kings.

Whether you eat or drink, or whatever you do, do all to the glory of God. (1 Cor. 10:31)

And whatever you do in word or deed, do all in the name of the Lord Jesus, giving thanks to God the Father through Him. (Col. 3:17)

In Jesus' parable of the great feast (Luke 14:16–24), it appears that the one concern of the servant was to fulfill the master's desire. It was grievous for him to report, "I have done as you commanded, and yet there is room!" He wanted to honor his master's wishes for

a banquet hall filled with guests. Are you tending to your stewardship with your Master's best interest at heart?

*Principle 2: We are to be good stewards of our home, church,
state, body, soul, and spirit.* To perform adequately, every steward
must know the realm of his responsibility. As we have already seen,
the Lord does not hold us accountable for what He has not
entrusted to our care. But He will call us into account for what He
has given us to oversee. There are six arenas in which we are given
specific stewardship responsibilities: our home, church, state, body,
soul, and spirit.

STEWARDSHIP AT HOME

God expects members of His Kingdom Family to look well to
the affairs of the home. Husbands and fathers are reminded that "if
anyone does not provide for his own, and especially for those of his
household, he has denied the faith and is worse than an unbeliever"
(1 Tim. 5:8). Wives and mothers are challenged by the example of
the virtuous woman who "looks well to the ways of her household"
(Prov. 31:27 NASB). Stewardship begins at home. It is the laboratory
of life where the principles of God are put to the test, proven true,
and exemplified for the generations to come.

STEWARDSHIP IN THE CHURCH

God's plan is for the ministry of the church to move forward
with the tithes, offerings, and sacrificial giving brought by each
member. As New Testament believers, our commitment should at
least exceed those who lived under the law rather than grace. They
were to "bring all the tithes [the first, or set-aside tenth] into the
storehouse" (Mal. 3:10). Paul's commendation to the churches in
Galatia are instructive. They brought their offerings "on the first
day of the week" (1 Cor. 16:2). These same people found giving to
be a joyful privilege because they "first gave their own selves to the
Lord" (2 Cor. 8:5 KJV). Once you have settled that Jesus is Lord of
all, giving to the church becomes a matter of simple and joyous
submission to His will.

STEWARDSHIP WITHIN THE STATE

Being members of God's Kingdom Family does not exempt us from responsibilities to our government. Paul exhorts us to "be subject unto the higher powers. For there is no power but of God: the powers that be are ordained of God" (Rom. 13:1 KJV). Then, after reminding us in verse 4 that government is "the minister of God to (us) for good," he echoes the words of Christ: "Render therefore to all their dues: tribute to whom tribute is due; custom to whom custom; fear to whom fear; honour to whom honour" (Rom. 13:7 KJV). We are to be good citizens and good stewards, faithfully fulfilling our responsibilities to our government and bringing honor to our Lord in the process.

STEWARDSHIP OF THE BODY

We also must consider the importance of stewardship over our physical bodies. (I am not suggesting a specific sequence by placing this here. However, I do know of those who have no balance in this area, either totally ignoring the importance of physical well-being or spending hours in the gym to the detriment of their family, church, or other responsibilities.) Your physical body has been entrusted to you by God and should be used for His glory. It is, after all, "the temple of the Holy Spirit" and you are exhorted to "glorify God in your body and in your spirit, which are God's" (1 Cor. 6:19–20).

STEWARDSHIP OF THE SOUL

Your soul (intellect, will, and emotions) is given you as a sacred trust and is to be used with the utmost care. We are urged to guard our hearts diligently for "out of it are the issues (or the boundaries you set) of life" (Prov. 4:23 KJV). Computer programmers use the term GIGO (garbage in, garbage out) to indicate that you can't get accurate information out of a computer unless it has been programmed accurately in the first place. Jesus said that even our speech has its source in "abundance of the heart" (Matt. 12:34; Luke 6:45). Little wonder that we are to be good stewards over our souls.

STEWARDSHIP OF THE SPIRIT

Again Paul's reminder to the Corinthian believers is worth noting: "Therefore glorify God in your body *and in your spirit* (emphasis mine), which are God's" (1 Cor. 6:20b). Rather than giving place to those things that hinder communion with our Master, our worship and praise of Him, we should commit to those things that will make us strong in spirit. Our only hope of success in spiritual warfare is to "be strong in the Lord and in the power of His might" (Eph. 6:10).

These are the six arenas in which God requires us to be faithful stewards. Have you given serious thought to the manner in which you are exercising your stewardship over them? Have you willingly accepted this assignment from God?

Principle 3: God has designated specific methods by which we can successfully fulfill our stewardship responsibilities. God never asks us to assume a responsibility without providing the means by which we may succeed. The following six methods are biblical, proven, and effective in times of financial crisis as well as prosperity.

A RIGHTEOUS LIFE

It only stands to reason that God would make His resources available to those who are, above all, committed to living a life that is pleasing to Him. After all, which of us would willingly entrust our own resources to someone harboring rebellion or resentment in his heart? A friend of mine says that the key to successful leadership is winning the heart of a man, not just his hand. God told King Asa, "The eyes of the LORD run to and fro throughout the whole earth, to show Himself strong on behalf of those whose heart is loyal to Him" (2 Chron. 16:9). As one man said, "The best commentary on the Scripture is a holy life."

> By humility and the fear of the LORD are riches and
> honor and life. (Prov. 22:4)

> Seek first the kingdom of God and His righteousness,
> and all these things shall be added to you. (Matt. 6:33)

> Trust in the LORD, and do good; dwell in the land,
> and feed on His faithfulness. Delight yourself also in the
> LORD, and He shall give you the desires of your heart.
> (Ps. 37:3–4)

When seeking to practice a stewardship that gains God's approval, start with a heart fully committed to Him. Is yours?

A DEVOTIONAL LIFE

When struggling over resources, many people overlook the essential nature of a consistent devotional life, prayer, and Bible study. It is in our devotional times, however, that we hear our Master's instructions and discover how to respond to Him.

> The effective, fervent prayer of a righteous man
> avails much. (James 5:16b)

> Ask, and it will be given to you; seek, and you will
> find; knock, and it will be opened to you. For everyone
> who asks receives, and he who seeks finds, and to him
> who knocks it will be opened. (Matt. 7:7–8)

> If you abide in Me, and My words abide in you, you
> will ask what you desire, and it shall be done for you.
> (John 15:7)

Are you practicing a life of consistent Bible reading, study, and prayer?

A DILIGENT LIFE

Sometimes people think that all they must do to receive from God is pray. Yet, God's Word tells us that, in a spirit of prayer, we are to diligently cooperate with God in our work.

> The labor of the righteous leads to life. (Prov. 10:16a)

> He who tills his land will be satisfied with bread, but
> he who follows frivolity is devoid of understanding.
> (Prov. 12:11)

> The soul of a sluggard desires, and has nothing;
> but the soul of the diligent shall be made rich.
> (Prov. 13:4)

And whatever he *does* shall prosper.

(Ps. 1:3, emphasis mine)

Are you both dedicated to the Lord and diligent in whatever your hand finds to do?

A GIVING LIFE

It seems impossible that giving away what God has entrusted to me actually makes even greater resources available. Yet that is God's plan; subtraction always precedes multiplication!

When we tithe (the first, set-aside tenth of all God entrusts to us), we find the windows of heaven will be opened.

> "Bring all the tithes into the storehouse,
> That there may be food in My house,
> And prove Me now in this,"
> Says the LORD of hosts,
> "If I will not open for you the windows of heaven
> And pour out for you such blessing
> That there will not be room enough to receive it."
> (Mal. 3:10)

When we give above and beyond the tithe, we will discover that God turns our lives into a channel through which He can pour even more of His blessings. "Give, and it will be given to you: good measure, pressed down, shaken together, and running over will be put into your bosom. For with the same measure that you use, it will be measured back to you" (Luke 6:38; see also Exod. 35–26; 1 Chron. 29; 2 Cor. 8; Phil. 4:10; Acts 4:32–37; Prov. 11:24–25).

A DISCIPLINED LIFE

Good stewards are always disciplined. They have learned to limit their desires, to live within their means. They want to live so that when God speaks they will not have to say, "But I'm already tied down. My resources are already committed." If you can come to the place in your walk with God where all you want is all God wants for you, then all your life you'll have all you want. And He will have all He wants of you! The key, of course, is getting to that point!

Better is a little with the fear of the LORD, than great treasure with trouble. (Prov. 15:16)

Not that I speak in regard to need, for I have learned in whatever state I am, to be content: I know how to be abased, and I know how to abound. (Phil. 4:11–12)

Godliness with contentment is great gain. (1 Tim. 6:6)

Are you practicing the principle of a disciplined life? Have you learned the meaning of contentment?

A DISCERNING LIFE

Members of God's Kingdom Family often discover that God has unusual ways of bringing the world's resources under their stewardship. It is imperative to seek the Lord's will in regard to their use, making sure that you are operating in concert with His will. God will never ask you to compromise with the world. As far as He is concerned, you will never be urged to violate a small principle for a big cause.

In Exodus 12:3 we read how the Egyptians complied with the Israelites' request for silver, gold, and other precious substances. Later these substances were used in the construction of the tabernacle in the wilderness.

In Genesis 30 we read the story of Jacob's prosperity while working for his father-in-law, Laban. By diligent stewardship of his resources, Jacob earned God's favor in spite of Laban's attempts to bring him into subjection.

Like the Israelites and like Jacob, a good steward realizes that when we are "wise as serpents and harmless as doves" the Lord will work on our behalf to make His resources available to us. They will come to us as we properly, honestly, and responsibly tap resources for which the world had other plans. Are you practicing the discernment of a good steward?

PRINCIPLES OF RESTORATION

Perhaps as you have examined God's principles for exercising wise stewardship you have become increasingly aware that you are living in violation of them. If so, you are probably already paying a price for your disobedience. God's way is always best! There are no extenuating circumstances that justify abandoning God's plan for your own. So how can you experience a genuine restoration to God and His way? His Word is not silent!

Principle 1: Restoration always begins with repentance. Repentance is not simply an attitude; it is an action. It is preceded by confession, agreeing with what God says about our sin. To confess means literally "to say along with." Confessing our sin means that we agree with God that we have sinned in specific ways. When we confess our sins, "He is faithful and just to forgive us our sins and to cleanse us from all unrighteousness" (1 John 1:9). This enables us to enjoy restored fellowship with the Lord.

Repentance, on the other hand, means to do an about-face, turning away from sin and toward God. To be frank, you have not repented of any sin you are still committing. If you are still practicing poor stewardship, you may have confessed to that reality but you have yet to repent. Repentance is a critical issue, essential for restoration. "He who covers his sins will not prosper [or, make progress], but whoever *confesses* and *forsakes* them will have mercy" (Prov. 28:13, emphasis mine).

Have you both confessed and repented of the sins associated with your poor stewardship? What steps are you taking that give evidence to your repentance?

Principle 2: Tithing and giving must become a way of life. Through tithing and giving—not indiscriminate giving, but in obedience to the Lord's leadership—you invite God into your financial situation. Tithing is not simply a matter for those "under the Law." Its practice proceeded the giving of the Law (see Gen. 12:20) and was commended by Christ (see Luke 11:42). Tithing results in both "blessing" and protection from the "devourer." These are necessary if you are to experience a restoration to God and to His participation in your recovery.

A friend of mine once candidly admitted that he struggled with both the precept of tithing (the first ten percent to the local church) and thus the practice of tithing. He said, "To be honest, I simply do not make enough money to go around. There are bills to pay, food and clothing for my family, and all the usual expenses. Then there are the unexpected situations that always seem to rise at the most inopportune times. There's nothing left after all these expenses, so how can I tithe?"

I explained to him that the tithe should be his first concern and that this would invite the Lord's blessing on his finances. Some time later he approached me with a sheepish smile. "Where have I been all my life?" he lamented. Then he explained that for several months he had been practicing the principle of tithing. "It's amazing!" he exclaimed. "All the bills are paid, and we actually have been able to place money in savings for the first time in our married life!" My friend was experiencing the restoration that comes from repentance!

Principle 3: Eliminating nonessentials shortens the journey. Many people are saddened by their financial situation but unwilling to eliminate the practices that got them there! Often one of those practices is the accumulation of things that might properly be called nonessential. These are things that are enjoyable but unnecessary, especially for someone who is on a journey out of financial distress.

In reality, it is theft to retain something in your possession while overdue in your payments to a creditor simply because you enjoy owning and using it. We are exhorted not to "withhold good from those to whom it is due, when it is in the power of your hand to do so" (Prov. 3:27). Eliminating nonessentials can be an exciting exercise, bringing a new discipline to your life as well as a new sense of contentment. After all, "godliness with contentment is great gain" (1 Tim. 6:6).

Principle 4: Your creditors need to know you care. No one likes to face people to whom they are in debt. Perhaps this is why it is said that "the quickest way to make an enemy out of a friend is to lend him money!" But if you have found yourself a victim of your own poor choices, it is better to approach your creditors before they are forced to approach you. Seek to work out a system of payment that is manageable yet evidences your desire to repay them as quickly as possible. It may mean great sacrifice, but it will be worth the pain to eliminate the encumbrance.

Remember that "the integrity of the upright shall guide them: but the perverseness of transgressors shall destroy them" (Prov. 11:3 KJV). And be sure to seek wise counsel. "Every purpose is established by counsel: and with good advice make war" (Prov. 20:18 KJV).

Principle 5: Restoration requires patience. It is amazing how impatient we are to solve problems that often have been years in the making. Recovering from the distress caused by unwise stewardship most often takes time and patience. But where you are headed is more important than where you have been. Patiently pursuing God's plan will ultimately lead to complete restoration, recovery, and a renewed appreciation for your responsibility.

Impatience and discontent will inevitably lead to disobedience. Think of the pain experienced by the prodigal son who could not wait for what he wanted. "Better is the poor who walks in his integrity than one perverse in his ways, though he be rich" (Prov. 28:6). Be patient, or you will pay a high price for your lack of discipline. "The thoughts of the diligent tend only to plenteousness; but of every one that is hasty only to want" (Prov. 21:5 KJV).

God has a way out of the distress caused by unwise and unfaithful stewardship. Every Christian should make a concerted effort to be free from the kind of financial encumbrances that strangle usefulness, destroy effectiveness, and rob us of joy. Good stewardship is a practice God will give you the grace to employ if you will follow His principles of restoration.

THE REWARDS OF A WISE SERVANT

Our membership in God's Kingdom Family is neither gained nor maintained by our performance. God's Word is abundantly clear on this issue, reminding us that our salvation is "not of works, lest any man should boast" (Eph. 2:9). On the other hand, the Lord does bless our obedience to Him. Obedience is evidence of our faith and His lordship in our lives. This is particularly true in the realm of stewardship. Notice the four benefits, or rewards, for faithful stewardship:

Effectiveness in your labor—The labor of a wise and faithful steward results in rewards that far exceed those of the labor of the average individual who works with no thought of responsibility toward God. God's Word reminds us that "the blessing of the LORD makes one rich, and He adds no sorrow with it" (Prov. 10:22). Working in concert with God, as His steward, brings an effectiveness that far exceeds mere "success." God makes our work count! What a contrast to those who complain that they seem to be just spinning their wheels.

A stick of dynamite can be successfully detonated simply by lighting the fuse and tossing it into the air. The explosion produces heat, light, sound, and smoke. But minutes later there is little evidence of what took place. It was successfully detonated, but its impact was not effective. On the other hand, that same stick of dynamite, strategically placed in a quarry, can bring down tons of rock. Working in concert with God, doing what our Master desires where He places us, brings a genuine effectiveness to our lives.

A life that is pleasing to God—Every true child of God longs to please Him. Nothing is so pleasing to God as the exercise of our faith in Him. It blesses the heart of God when we take Him at His Word. "Without faith it is impossible to please Him, for he who comes to God must believe that He is, and that He is a rewarder of those who diligently seek Him" (Heb. 11:6). Wise and faithful stewards diligently seek out the Master's best interest then act accordingly.

As an officer in my university class, I had the responsibility of approaching the president of our school for permission to conduct a schoolwide fair as a fund-raiser. Being a lowly freshman, I approached him with some trepidation, realizing that he had far more important things to do than accommodate our seemingly frivolous plans. Imagine my surprise to discover that he was, in fact, honored by my appeal. He went out of his way to provide far more than I requested, telling me of his involvement years earlier in a similar event. What's more, we became friends. In fact, later, as a graduate student, I had the privilege of working under him as a teaching fellow. Similarly, God is honored and pleased by our appeals to His grace and our faithful compliance to His will.

The enjoyment of a remarkable abundance—Frequently I am approached by those who want to share their tithing testimony with me. As they recount how God brought them to understand the concept of tithing, and then to the faithful adherence to this principle of God, they inevitably tell how "it just doesn't add up on paper," but they now have more resources available than when they kept the tithe for themselves! Further, they will tell how God has "rebuked the devourer" according to His promise, and now they just get more use out of the things they purchase. Their expression of wise and faithful stewardship has placed them in the flow of God's economy.

A study of the biblical concept of *blessing* is enlightening. In reality, a blessing is a sovereign act of God by which He causes someone or something to produce supernaturally more than is naturally possible. God promises that a life of faithful obedience will be blessed. In Malachi 3:10–11, for instance, God promises those who faithfully bring their tithes to the storehouse that they will have the windows of heaven opened to them and a blessing poured out until there is no more need. Additionally, He promises to rebuke the "devourer," or the very things that eat up the resources He has entrusted to them.

Jesus (in Luke 6:38) says that those who give unselfishly will not end up with less but more! They will receive in return a blessing poured out with "good measure, pressed down, shaken together, and running over." This is simply another illustration of the remarkable abundance God makes available to those who practice wise and faithful stewardship.

Passing on a legacy of faith—Wise stewardship produces a legacy of faith. This is why "a good man leaves an inheritance to his children's children" (Prov. 13:22). The inheritance he leaves may consist of financial resources, but it is far more than that. He leaves a legacy of goodness. His name is a good name, which "is rather to be chosen than great riches" (Prov. 22:1 KJV).

Years ago a wealthy man was encouraged to give a generous gift to construct a great building on a college campus. Shortly after making the commitment, the stock market fell and he suffered a great financial loss. A friend chided him saying, "I'm sure you wish you hadn't given your money to that institution!" He responded by taking his friend out to see the building, noting that it provided for a ministry that would change the lives of many. "You see," said the wise steward, "everything I kept for myself, I lost. But everything I gave away, I still have!" Here was a man who was leaving a legacy of faith.

Are you enjoying the benefits of effective labor? Do you sense that your life is pleasing to God? Are you blessed with remarkable abundance? Are you building a legacy of faith that will live long after you? If you can answer yes to these questions, then you are experiencing the rewards of wise stewardship. But there is more! One day in eternity, you will hear your Master say, "Well done, good and faithful servant!"

Thinking It Through, Living It Out

1. Based on God's principles of stewardship, how would you currently rate yourself? A wise steward? Struggling? An unwise steward? How do you think God sees your stewardship? Do you live with the awareness that He will, one day, require an accounting for the manner in which you have overseen all He has entrusted to your care? Will you discuss the issue of stewardship with your family?

2. What has God placed in your care so that you might exercise stewardship over it? What abilities? Resources? Relationships? Opportunities? Have you seen these as belonging to

God and only entrusted to your stewardship? Have you thought of these as your own? Have you sought to glorify God by the manner in which you have handled what He has entrusted to you? How can your family glorify God by wise stewardship? What practical steps can you take to give evidence that He is Lord of all?

3. Have you sought to be a steward whose life is characterized by righteousness? Do you have a consistent devotional life? Are you diligent in your work? Do you practice tithing? Giving? In what way do you seek to limit your desires so that the resources entrusted to you might be even more available for God's use? Do you ask God for discernment in your use of resources made available through worldly sources? Is your family using its resources to expand God's kingdom?

4. Are you in distress because of poor stewardship? What steps are you taking to resolve these difficulties? Are they in accord with God's principles of restoration? Did you begin your pilgrimage out of bondage by confessing your poor stewardship and practicing repentance? What progress are you making? If you have not started already, will you begin today by taking the appropriate steps toward restoration? What steps can your family take to correct any effects of poor stewardship?

5. Are you experiencing the rewards of wise stewardship? Do you understand that these rewards make it possible for you to continue practicing your stewardship at a new and exciting level? In what ways has God truly blessed you? Your family? Your work? Do you and your family take time regularly to thank God for these blessings? Do you consider how they may be used to reach others for Christ?

The greatest and most noble purpose in life is to glorify the Lord through the fulfillment of His Great Commission. I will glorify the Lord by sharing my faith with my family and by joining with them and others in specific activities that cultivate a passion for fulfilling the Great Commission (Matt. 28:19–20; Acts 1:8; John 4:38–39; Rom. 1:16; 1 Tim. 5:8; Rev. 22:17; Rom. 1:16).

CHAPTER EIGHT

SHARING THE GOSPEL OF JESUS CHRIST

W hat is the one characteristic that most distinguishes those who are members of God's Kingdom Family? To put it into the words of the Kingdom Family Commitment, they are, above all, characterized by a "passion for fulfilling the Great Commission." They view life with an eye for sharing the gospel.

Bob and Peggy Oxford live in Denver, Colorado, where they are members of the dynamic Applewood Baptist Church. Bob is a petroleum engineer, a businessman, and founder of Industrial Gas Services, a nationwide consulting firm. For the past few years Peggy has worked beside him in this family owned and operated business. But while that is the Oxfords' business, it is not their life. Their life is consumed with a passion to use everything God has provided to them as a means for sharing the gospel and encouraging others to do the same.

Several times a year the Oxfords have participated together in short-term overseas mission projects where they have been joined by their children and most recently their grandchildren. Their two children are also strong believers in Christ, serving faithfully in their church. The Oxfords are faithful in the outreach programs of their local church and have served in various ministry capacities both locally and nationally. But their favorite responsibilities relate to the mission endeavors of their church. Their home has been opened to countless visitors, both nationals and foreigners, who have found a warm-hearted welcome and an eagerness to talk about Jesus. International students and business people, many of whom they have personally led to Christ, are their favorites. They keep up with them, visit and correspond with them, even though the list grows by the month.

During the fifty years of their married life, the Oxfords have sought to be careful stewards of the resources entrusted to them, determined to make them count for Christ's sake and the kingdom's. They make every attempt to keep what God has given them in circulation for the fulfillment of the Great Commission. Recently, while participating with them in an overseas partnership crusade, we found ourselves dining with a renowned military general with whom they have cultivated a friendship based on a mutual desire to spread the gospel. Never offensive, always gracious and ready to share their faith, the Oxfords picture what is meant by a Kingdom Family.

THE UNIQUE DISTINCTION

Perhaps the most unique attribute distinguishing members of God's Kingdom Family is their consistent eagerness to share the gospel with others—their own family, their neighbors, their work or school associates, and people around the world. They are motivated by something more than Christ's command, although that certainly is sufficient for any soldier. They operate from an inner compulsion born out of their own experience with Christ and the new nature that has resulted from it. They have a love for Him and an eagerness for others to possess what they have—forgiveness of sin, peace with God, and genuine purpose, not to mention eternal life.

Even if they are the only believer in their home or workplace, this personal experience with Christ changes the atmosphere where they live and work. To put it simply: Christ, living in them, begins to reach out to others through them. It is not through some kind of unfeeling, mechanical carrying out of His Commission that the people around them are attracted to Christ. Instead, they become recipients of Christ's pure, sincere love and concern for them. It is the work of the Holy Spirit through the life of a believer, a winsome drawing of people to the Master.

The impact of this life as a member of God's Kingdom Family is powerfully illustrated by a friend of mine, a fellow church member who believed in Christ only a few years ago yet is being used of God to bring many to Him. Originally alone in his family as a believer, he has subsequently been joined by his wife, then his two children and his mother.

Eager to remove a heavy bondage of debt that required his wife to work many hours outside the home, he took a second job doing night deliveries for a local pizza chain. The Holy Spirit prompted him to add something to his deliveries, the story of his personal conversion to Christ. Once the delivery was made and payment was received, he asked, "Could I leave with you the story of my life?" Upon receiving an affirmative reply, he would hand them "his story," which he had typed and copied.

Imagine our surprise when we began to receive calls at church from people wanting to know just how they could find what their deliveryman called his "new life." Later we discovered that he had placed our church phone number at the bottom of the page! This is God's Spirit at work in one man's life.

If an individual is blessed to be part of a physical family that is also committed to Kingdom Family principles, this eagerness to share the gospel is encouraged and cultivated at every age. It is my prayer that God will generate a Kingdom Family movement among true believers everywhere, a movement in which it is acknowledged that there is no more winsome or compelling argument for the gospel than the way the life of Christ is powerfully demonstrated by an entire family; a movement in which at birth, families say, "This child is created for God's glory and His service"; a movement in which, on a regular basis, the family discusses how best they may live out God's principles and serve Him, however and wherever in the world He leads; a movement in which all family members are involved in either going, helping go, or letting go!

Many families are seeing that the primary training for missions and evangelism rightly takes place in the home. Recently I called the home of a church member to share some information with her husband. "Pastor," the man's wife said almost in a whisper, "I apologize, but I'm right in the middle of conducting a Bible study with some ladies from my neighborhood! Do you know about my Bible study?" I confessed my joy and surprise. After our conversation was completed, I thought, *Now there's another Kingdom Family!* Like others, they were using their home as a mission station and modeling the principle for their children.

Kingdom Families have the world on their heart! In the church I am privileged to serve as pastor, new members are urged to get and maintain a current passport. We believe that few things can so expand the vision of a believer as personal participation in overseas missions. This emphasis on missions is best nurtured in a home where, early on, children are taught to pray, give, and expect to participate in sharing the gospel around the world. Family nights for Bible study, prayer, and planning for participation in Kingdom Family projects are a growing trend among evangelicals. Mission boards are encouraging family participation in short-term projects. Students—both men and women and starting in their teens—are encouraged to become personally involved in missions. More parents are rearing their children with the assumption that a portion of their early years will be spent in specific involvement in missions.

Keeping a Kingdom Family focus requires a clear understanding of what it means to give sacrificially of both ourselves and our resources. This is one of the big life lessons children learn best through personal example. Mission projects can help the concept of a sacrificial lifestyle become a reality. These projects should be significant enough that real lifestype changes must take place in order for them to be successfully completed. After all, if you can still live, wear, go, spend, drive, and eat in the same manner as before, then nothing has been sacrificed! Sacrifice requires an alteration in our lifestyle; something is given up for God's higher cause.

A growing number of families are seeing the value of a family mission trip. This enables them to plan and pray together as they anticipate their days on the field. Together they begin to set aside resources for the trip, praying all the time that the Lord will bless their days in His harvest field. Giving up vacation time for such a trip becomes part of the sacrifice and only adds value and significance to the time they will spend together. What better memories could a family have than those of their shared experiences on mission with God? But get prepared! Family mission trips often become the breeding ground for future service!

Kingdom Families keep the mission fire burning brightly through involvement in their local church's Great Commission ministries. As a family they pray, give, go, and help others go into every corner of their world. Prayer is most effective when it is specific. Many families include missionary families in their regular prayer times together. They communicate with them and pray according to their specific needs.

Underlying all that a Kingdom Family does in regard to missions, both local and international, is the growing assumption that, somehow and in some way, every family member will participate in fulfilling the Great Commission. They have learned to look beyond their own comforts to the ultimate, eternal harvest that is to come. And they face the possibility of God's call to a lifetime of missions with a sense of joyful eagerness. Jeannie and I have had the privilege of serving with our children on both short- and long-term mission opportunities. Now we look on with joy as they lead their own children to a similar desire for sharing the gospel, both at home and overseas.

THE DRIVING FORCE

What is the driving force behind the Kingdom Family movement? Members of God's Kingdom Family have a firm grasp on four heart-stirring issues. These issues are clearly spelled out in Proverbs 24:10–12. We'll look at each in detail; but first, read carefully the following passage:

> If you faint in the day of adversity,
> Your strength is small.
> Deliver those who are drawn toward death,
> And hold back those stumbling to the slaughter.
> If you say, "Surely we did not know this,"
> Does not He who weighs the hearts consider it?
> He who keeps your soul, does He not know it?
> And will He not render to each man according to his
> deeds?

Compelling realities—Members of God's Kingdom Family believe with all their heart that there is no greater peril than for a person to be without Christ. While they also believe that there can be no more liberating experience than knowing Christ by faith, they are keenly aware that, without Christ, a person is genuinely and eternally lost.

Being drawn unto death pictures the unbeliever as a blind man who has been taken by the hand and led along. In this instance, it is the adversary who has taken their hand. And their destiny is not life but death, eternal death. Apart from Holy Spirit intervention, they will die in their trespasses and sins. Their plight touches the heart of God, who sends divine intervention in the person of His Holy Spirit and in His Kingdom Family members.

But there's more to this lostness experienced by those without Christ. Apart from Christ they have no hope. They are on the edge of the precipice. The soil is giving way beneath them. All that is needed to send them over the edge is one push forward or simply no one reaching out to help.

Years ago I sat riveted by a photograph in a local newspaper. In an attempt to portray the ravages of a flood in a nearby state, they showed a picture of a desperate rescue attempt. A man was being swept downstream to certain death. On the shore, another was reaching out with a stick, urging the man to grab hold. But you could see from the distance between them and the look of panic on the victim's face that it was too little too late. In seconds he would be drowned.

A lady came to one of our worship services one night having just witnessed a similar experience. She had been to an air show at a local airport. During a skydiving exhibition, a man's parachute had failed to deploy; then his emergency chute was tangled. She said that the man had fallen near her, so near that she had witnessed the look on his face before the deadly impact. "It was a look of utter hopelessness, and I will never forget it," she related. What a picture of the plight of any person who fails to trust Christ! Hopelessly lost!

These of whom the writer of Proverbs speaks are being drawn unto "death"! Kingdom Family members know that the eternal destiny of those without Christ is a place the Bible calls hell. Hell is more than an actual place; it is both an *awful* place and an *always* place. In other words, there is never a moment when an individual, having once entered hell, can say, "I am almost finished with this experience." And there's never a moment when the senses cease being impacted, a moment when an individual can say, "I'm getting accustomed to this horror!" When Kingdom Family members reflect on what God has saved them *from* as well as what He has saved them *to,* they eagerly anticipate the joy of sharing God's good news with their own family members and friends.

Critical responsibilities—In light of these compelling realities, members of God's Kingdom Family are led to two critical responsibilities related to the Great Commission. We must seek, above all, to rescue people from the impending judgment of God. And if they reject Christ, it must be in spite of our attempts rather than because we never tried to share the gospel with them.

Some years ago one of the most fierce tornadoes in America's history swept through our town, only narrowly missing our church! I had gathered in the church building with my family, neighboring families, and other church members to escape the pending storm. Once the winds died down, we came out to survey the devastation. Knowing that many people, including many of our own were trapped in the rubble, we immediately mounted a search-and-rescue effort.

I will never forget that night! We ran, stumbling over the debris, shouting, "Is anyone in there? Does anyone need help?" Later, as some of us were trying to get strength for a second effort, I looked at our little band of rescuers. No one had given a thought to what they were wearing or what the effort would do to our clothing. Formality was irrelevant in this attempt! We were desperate because we knew lives were at stake. That's the way Kingdom Family members feel about people without Christ. They are helpless and in need of rescue at any cost! After all, Jesus has already given His life for them.

What about those who simply refuse the message of the gospel? Do we have any responsibility regarding them? In the New American Standard Proverbs 24:11 reads, "And those who are staggering to slaughter, Oh hold them back." In other words, God is saying, "If they will not be rescued, you should at least restrain them!" In other words, if they do choose the path to hell, they should at least have to overcome our efforts to get there. Or, as one man said, "They may fall into the pit, but we will be clutching at the laces of their shoes!" The fact that you are a family member or friend of someone without Christ cannot guarantee that they will trust in Him. But it should give them an advantage!

Callous reactions—One of the great benefits of being linked with other members of God's Kingdom Family is that it brings the joy of shared experiences and the encouragement of shared accountability. We have others who see our blind spots and challenge us to be at our best. Their contribution, along with prayer and the study of God's Word, are indispensable benefits afforded every member of God's family. The writer of Proverbs warns of three reactions we must avoid as we seek to fulfill the Great Commission.

First, we must not "faint" or decline to become involved in this great work to which He has invited, commanded, and commissioned us. We all have heard of those who have said as if they truly believe it is the case, "Witnessing, or leading people to Christ, is simply not my gift." Imagine any soldier responding to his superior's command in a similar fashion. "Sorry Colonel, you're the greatest, and I have utmost respect for you, but this fighting is not my gift."

I know people who, in an attempt to sound spiritual, say that they wait to feel a "burden" before they share their faith. Nowhere in our Lord's Commission is there even a hint about the necessity of having some kind of feeling in order to witness effectively. As a matter of fact, I have found it to be the other way around. Faithfully discharging our responsibilities to God seems to have a positive effect on our feelings.

Second, we must not delay, or "forbear." My mother often said, "Delayed obedience is disobedience." Can the Lord feel anything less about our own reluctance to obey the prompting of His Spirit? One of the great sorrows of my own life revolves around an encounter with a future student in the university I attended. He said at the end of a swimming session that I was coaching, "You're a preacher, aren't you?" When I replied in the affirmative, he continued, "I've been thinking a lot about eternity and God." Weary from the day's activities, I replied, "Yeah? Well you and I will have to talk about that some day." That was a conversation I fully intended to have. Upon returning to school a few days afterward, I inquired about him, only to discover that, just the day before, he had taken his own life. I know he is responsible for his own choices, but I also know that I delayed in choosing to obey God myself.

Third, we cannot dispute the issue with God, saying, "Behold, we knew it not." In other words, God knows what we know, and we know He has called us to be His witnesses. When our family was living in Zimbabwe, Africa, I had a dispute with God over a specific witnessing responsibility. As I was preparing to preach at a retreat, God reminded me of a blind man who sat each day on the streets of our town. I had intended to share Christ with him, but it never seemed just the right time. Besides that, in order to share with him, I would have to sit down with him there on the busy sidewalk. Looking back, I am ashamed at the utter wickedness and rebellion of my heart. Think of it! I had come seven thousand miles to be a missionary, and now I wouldn't even go a few feet to follow my Master. God just broke my heart in the midst of that dispute, and before the day was over, my friend became my brother. Having a dispute with God is futile. Or as a friend of mine once said, "You don't have arms long enough to box with God!"

A certain reckoning—Kingdom Family members know that one day they will stand before Christ, not in the final, or great white throne judgment, but at the judgment seat of Christ (2 Cor. 5:10; Rom. 14:10). The issue will not be whether we will be in heaven (We would not be at this judgment without the assurance of eternity with Christ!), but what we did with what was given us.

The writer of Proverbs clearly states that this judgment is both accurate and assured. "Does not He who weighs the heart consider it? He who keeps your soul, does He not know it?" (24:12). With those words he speaks to the absolute accuracy of this coming judgment for all believers. At this judgment we will be confronted with our stewardship over that which the Lord entrusted to our care, not just material resources but opportunities as well. The Lord who "ponders the heart" will be the judge.

Is this judgment really going to take place? "Will He not render to each man according to his deeds?" (Prov. 24:12). No room is left for us to think otherwise. It is certain that one day we will stand before the Lord and render up an account. Our works will be tried as by fire, says the apostle Paul (1 Cor. 3:12–15), and the truth will be known. It will be revealed whether we have built with "wood, hay, straw," or "gold, silver, precious stones." This is why Kingdom Family members not only share their faith with their family and friends but also "join with others in specific projects which create a passion for fulfilling the Great Commission."

What an incredible privilege it is to be a member of God's Kingdom Family! But it is a privilege that must be shared. After all, God's Kingdom Family must be extended "until the Lord comes"!

Thinking It Through, Living It Out

1. Take a test! How eager are you to share with others the good news of Jesus? What excuses have you offered for not being faithful in your witness? Have you ever personally led someone to a saving knowledge of Christ? How long ago was that experience? Have you been willing to train so that you might be more effective in your witness?

2. Is each member of your family a believer in Christ? Have you shared Christ with each member of your family? Sometimes family members can seem the most difficult to approach with the gospel. Why do you think that is? Have you asked God to help you overcome your fear? Is there some apology, some forgiveness, some issue that needs to be resolved before you can share Christ with your family? Will you resolve it?

3. Have you contemplated the eternal destiny of people without Christ? Have you considered the possibility of mission service, either short- or long-term? Have you discussed this possibility with your family? How are you and your family participating now in missions? If you are a parent, how willing are you for your children to answer a specific call of God to a career in mission service? If you are a senior adult or retired, have you made yourself available to God for mission service?

4. What evidences exist in your life that you have sacrificed "for the gospel's sake?" Do you keep aware of current mission opportunities? Subscribe to a missions journal? How often do you actually pray for missionaries? Are you personally acquainted with missionaries? Correspond with them?

5. What specific steps are you willing to take to develop a Kingdom Family atmosphere in your home? Will you talk with the other family members who live with you? Will you set aside an evening a week to pray with them, to study God's Word? Discuss your family's involvement in the Great Commission? Plan a project that will help you move beyond your comfort zone in sharing the gospel?

CHAPTER NINE

YOU CAN BUILD A KINGDOM FAMILY

You can build a Kingdom Family. Whoever you are and in whatever circumstances you may presently find yourself, it is possible for you to become a member of God's Kingdom Family and to begin building a Kingdom Family according to God's blueprint. Each week, when the congregation I am privileged to pastor gathers for worship, I am assured of the truth of that promise. Our church is filled with individuals and families whose lives are testimonies to the grace of God. That grace enables us to live out Kingdom Family principles.

Meet Pete and Debbie Livingston who are building a Kingdom Family. They seem always to find their place in worship, on the second row of the second section to my left. That wasn't always the case, however, as both would tell you. Pete and Debbie were on the fast track to success in their respective careers when suddenly they found themselves in such moral and marital disarray that divorce seemed certain. Praying friends in their church convinced Pete to stand for his family. Taking drastic steps, including the discipline of reshaping their priorities, severing ties that were dragging them into divorce, and recommitting themselves to Christ's lordship in their lives, Pete and Debbie began to rebuild their marriage and family.

In addition to the two children born to their marriage, they have since adopted five others—one of Hispanic decent, one from a mixed-race union, two from Cambodia, and one from Bulgaria. In addition to his outside consulting service, Pete serves part-time as a minister to families in our church. He and Debbie have teamed up to form Radically Married, a teaching ministry that has reached more than three thousand people through our church and countless others in additional venues. With missions on their heart, Pete and Debbie travel frequently to minister in foreign countries. Their eldest son will soon graduate from college and begin training for overseas ministry. The Livingstons are a Kingdom Family.

So is the family of Trey and Brenda Palmer. When not in the choir, they usually are seated with their children in the second section back and to my right as I face the congregation. Trey and Brenda had the privilege of growing up in strong Christian families, active in their respective churches. From the beginning, Trey and Brenda dedicated their family, which now includes five children, to the Lord.

Over the past several years, Trey, an environmental specialist and deacon in our church, has become increasingly concerned about the trend away from family values in our community. Recently his concern, coupled with his strong biblical convictions, led him into the political arena where he sought office as a state representative. In spite of being the first African-American to run for that position on his party's ticket, and in spite of running against a firmly entrenched incumbent, Trey, Brenda, their family, and their church family saw his campaign as a means of bringing key issues to the surface.

Although he lost this first political bid (Those on both sides of the aisle in our church family still think he was the best candidate!), his clear enunciation of the issues brought notice and admiration throughout our community, including an endorsement by the local paper. So what did his family do the week following a hard-fought election? They were in their places in church—choir, Bible study, missions, Scripture memory organizations, and student ministry. The Palmers are a Kingdom Family.

As you have seen with the Livingstons and Palmers, Kingdom Families come in all shapes, sizes, ages, and stages in life. They have learned to overcome, even when things do not turn out the way they might hope. Charleta Garner sings in our church choir, teaches, visits in our evangelism ministry, teaches Spanish as a second language, attends our 5:30 morning prayer each day, spends Tuesdays and Thursdays sharing the gospel in our benevolence ministry (especially with the Spanish speaking), and constantly encourages her pastor. Such an active life is not easy for this seventy-eight-year-old former missionary whose husband died of Alzheimer's disease three years ago.

"One day this old lady is going to go down," Charleta said to me one day when I asked why a retired missionary would enroll in evangelism training, "and I want to go down like a big rock, making lots of waves and dragging others into God's kingdom with me!" Although living alone, she is scarcely alone. Her house is often filled with guests and family members, some of whom also are serving overseas on the mission field. When others would have excused themselves, Charleta considers herself under orders from her King; she continues to reach out to her world as a member of God's Kingdom Family.

Reaching out is the name of the game for Ed and Shelby Nuckols, who sit almost directly in front of me each time we gather for worship. Shelby literally prayed Ed through and then out of his years of destructive addiction. It wasn't easy at first; there were good days and bad. Then Ed met Jesus, and everything changed. Together Ed and Shelby began to pick up the pieces of their marriage and reassemble them into a Kingdom Family.

Generally Ed and Shelby are surrounded with an unusual group of folks they look upon as their special sheep. As members of God's Kingdom Family, Ed and Shelby asked for and received a vision for an effective ministry to those seeking to overcome addictions. Every time I see them, it seems as if at least one member of their Overcomers Class is in tow. And our church family now has scattered through it those who, under their ministry, have gained

genuine victory. They know the value of prayer in the spiritual bat-
tles in which they are engaged. So whether it's our Wednesday Hour
of Power or the daily morning prayer, you can count on seeing Ed,
Shelby, and some of the sheep who comprise the Kingdom Family.

Recently, after visiting a new resident in a local nursing home,
I went back to the entry area to find Shirley Chapman, a nurse's aid
and Kingdom Family member. I knew Shirley would give this new
resident the kind of loving attention he so desperately needed at
the time. Shirley is single now, after years of living in a situation for
which the word *abusive* scarcely does justice. In addition, Shirley
was victim of an automobile accident that left her sometimes struggling with motor skills. Throughout this time, including days of
incredibly deep despair, Shirley has never lost her song and her
determination to praise the Lord in all things.

To be honest, Shirley and I don't always agree on what consti-
tutes appropriate praise and worship. But then, we don't have to
agree on everything because we do agree on the one thing that
counts: Jesus deserves our all. On the occasions when Shirley
seems to be "putting on" a little, I try to remind myself that, when
the weather is warm enough, I just might pass a street corner
where she has positioned herself in concert for all who pass by. And
I've grown accustomed to sharing with folks who are startled by
"that lady who walks through the church real fast, singing as she
goes," that she is simply our Shirley.

Rarely a week passes that Shirley doesn't hand me a note
requesting prayer for someone. As a member of God's Kingdom
Family, she faithfully employs the battle strategy that's enabled her
to go forward when it appeared all the world was against her. On
that morning I was glad God had a family member there in the
nursing home, ready to pour out loving support. "Hi, sweetheart,"
she said to the man. "You are just beautiful today!" She hugged the
patient, then turned to me and said, "You go on now, Brother Tom.
Everything will be all right."

Like the Palmers, Dr. Kevin Penwell and his wife, Sarah, grew
up in homes where they were loved, supported, and urged along in

their faith. Kevin's parents are faithful members of our church. They insert an incredible servant attitude into the atmosphere, regardless of where they are. Sarah's parents are equally involved in our church, both real experts when it comes to communicating about family issues. Sarah's father, a "completed Jew" and son of a Holocaust survivor, is one of the most articulate and gifted teachers I have ever known.

Having faithful and dedicated parents is no guarantee that the children will become the same, but it sure gives them an advantage. Kevin and Sarah have taken advantage of their heritage; and along with their three children, they are building a Kingdom Family of their own. As I write, Kevin is completing his last few months of medical residency and soon will begin a practice of his own. I am taken, however, by this couple's desire to live out the principles of a Kingdom Family.

Because I had the privilege of officiating at Kevin and Sarah's wedding, I also had the joy of guiding them through our church's premarital counseling. At every session I was impressed with their eagerness to live out their faith in some practical ways. Kevin, for instance, participated in overseas missions tours. In fact, working side by side on the mission field with another of our church's physicians, he fell in love with the medical practice and the doors for witness it opened. Sarah worked in our church office during the early days of their courtship, impressing everyone there with her enthusiasm for life and for the things of God.

It's easy to find excuses when you're in medical school. After all, the demands are seemingly overwhelming. Yet, if at all possible, Kevin and his family will be faithful in the ministries of their church, faithful in their support of missions, and eager to share the gospel with others. Generally, early on Tuesday mornings and even after a full night of emergency room rotation, Kevin will be at our men's Bible study and prayer meeting. As one of the youngest deacons in our church, his participation is both valuable and insightful. This is the Kingdom Family as it ought to be.

Unfortunately, many people don't have the advantages shared by Kevin and Sarah. Erica Maia could only dream of such family support. She is a first-year student at Oklahoma Baptist University. Erica's father is Brazilian, though her mother is from a Japanese family. As a result she speaks Portuguese, Japanese, and now English. Coming to the United States to complete high school, Erica was introduced to Christ by members of our church with whom she was staying. As a member of God's Kingdom Family, her hunger to grow spiritually led her to participate in our evangelism training for high school students. That training, and the spiritual nurture provided by her host family, made all the difference in her life.

Returning home to Japan for a brief visit, Erica had the privilege of leading first her mother and then her brother to Christ. Returning to the U.S. to complete her schooling, she continued to share her faith, seeing many of her friends come to Christ as well. Now with her parents' encouragement she is attending Oklahoma Baptist University where she is majoring in cross-cultural ministries and journalism.

No, eighteen-year-old Erica does not have the advantages shared by Kevin and Sara. But, as a member of God's Kingdom Family, she has determined to be the first in line of many generations to come, generations she believes will be mighty for the Lord. Often during our morning prayer, I look up to see Erica kneeling with her sponsor, Tuca Ogle, praying, I'm sure, for her own family and for those generations to come.

BY GOD'S GRACE YOU CAN DO IT!

Your story may not be identical to that of Erica, Kevin and Sarah, Shirley, Ed and Shelby, Charleta, Trey and Brenda, or Pete and Debbie, or any of the others you have met in the pages of this book. But you do have a story! Does your story reveal that you are a member of God's Kingdom Family? Does it show that you are committed to building your life on the Kingdom Family? Does it include your commitment to use the balance of your life sharing your faith with your family and joining with them and others in the kind of activities that cultivate a passion for fulfilling the Great Commission?

Heaven will be a wonderful place! But there is still much for us to do as members of God's family and citizens of His kingdom. As Amy Carmichael once wrote from the mission field in India, "We have all of eternity to celebrate our victories, but only a few minutes before sundown to win them."

You can do it! You can become a member of God's Kingdom Family! By God's grace you can build a Kingdom Family, starting right now, where you are. Welcome to God's Kingdom Family!

Thinking It Through, Living It Out

1. After reading this book, do you feel you have a good understanding of the phrase *Kingdom Family*? How would you describe a Kingdom Family? Are you a member of God's Kingdom Family, having by faith repented of your sin and believed in Christ alone for your salvation?

2. Every building has its foundation. A Kingdom Family rests on Seven Pillars. How many of those can you name? How committed are you to both the principles and the activities involved in building on these Seven Pillars? Are there any with which you struggle? Why do you think that is the case?

3. Throughout this book you have read the stories of members of God's Kingdom Family. What is your story? (An excellent resource for recording "your story" is found in the book *In Their Own Words* by this author and Dr. Robert G. Witty, Broadman & Holman, 2003). Are you convinced that, starting now, you can build a Kingdom Family? Why, or why not?

4. Are there any people who, by God's grace, cannot become members of the Kingdom Family? What would exclude them from this possibility? What would you say to someone who thinks he or she is beyond hope or help? How would

you respond to someone who agrees with the Seven Pillars but thinks his or her life is too far spent to employ these principles? Where would you suggest they start?

5. The ultimate purpose of a Kingdom Family is to glorify God and, as a result, draw people to Christ. Is that happening in your life? Through your family? What Great Commission projects are you and your family considering at present? Will you carry through on these? When will you start?

ABOUT THE AUTHOR

A former president of the Southern Baptist Convention and the SBC Pastor's Conference, Tom Elliff has led crusades and conferences across the United States and in many foreign countries. He is a graduate of Ouachita Baptist University and Southwestern Baptist Theological Seminary, serving earlier pastorates in Arkansas, Texas, Oklahoma, and Colorado. For two years the Elliffs were commissed by the Foreign Mission Board (now the International Mission Board) of the Southern Baptist Convention, and ministered in Zimbabwe, Africa. In addition to their church's radio and television ministry, the Elliffs have often been guests on nationwide broadcasts addressing family issues. Tom is currently chairing the Southern Baptist Council on Family Life.

Along with *Unbreakable! The Seven Pillars of a Kingdom Family*, Tom has been a contributing author to other publications including, *MasterLife*, the *Family Worship Bible*, and *The Disciple Study Bible*. He is the author of several books, including *Praying for Others* (B&H), *The Pathway to God's Presence* (B&H), *A Passion for Prayer* (Crossway), *Letters to Lovers* (B&H), and, along with Robert G. Witty, a coauthor of *In Their Own Words* (B&H).

A third generation Baptist pastor, Tom and his wife, Jeannie, reside in Oklahoma City, Oklahoma where for over seventeen years he has pastored the First Southern Baptist Church, Del City. They are the parents of four children and grandparents of eighteen grandchildren. Each of their children, and their children's families, is active in church ministry and missions.

OTHER AVAILABLE BROADMAN & HOLMAN TITLES BY TOM ELLIFF

Letters to Lovers (0-8054-2669-8)
(coauthored with his wife Jeannie)

Letters to Lovers gives good, godly advice on marriage and family relationships. The reader will find profound truth and penetrating realism in this heart-to-heart love letter that could only be written by a couple who have ministered to tens of thousands of marriages and families over the past three decades.

In Their Own Words (0-8054-2637-X)

In Their Own Words collects personal testimonies from a broad spectrum of Christian leaders, allowing the testimonies to speak for themselves. Over fifty testimonies are included from such diverse personalities as Bill and Vonette Bright, Charles Colson, James and Shirley Dobson, Elisabeth Elliot, Adrian Rogers, and Ed Young.